Welcome to You. *Defined!* This book was written with YOU in mind. It h~~~~ ~~~~~~~~~~ ~~~~~~~~~
to help you consciously participate in your life—to cut through the internal and external chaos,
clutter, and noise . . . to *Dare* to go within . . .to *Define* what you want . . . to show up as *YOU!*

From personal experience, we know that *who we are on the inside, is how we live, lead, and influence.*

It is our sincere hope that this book sparks an inside out connection for you, in a fashion that's
original and authentic to who you are—propelling you to be that—as an individual and as a
leader.

Alyssa & Cyndi

Amazing people do not *just* happen. Personal growth must be intentional. *Life is not about repeating yourself, it's about improving yourself.*

RED GLASSES MOVEMENT

Audrey Lou

live boldly. love big. pass it on.
redglassesmovement.org

On our journey of writing You. Defined! we discovered our friends at the Red Glasses
Movement, and wanted to highlight their mission of inspiring people all over the world to *live boldly, love big and pass it on.*

This inspirational movement was started in honor of a special 5-year-old girl, Audrey. Audrey
was defined by her bright Red Glasses, her crushing hugs and uninhibited determination! When
Audrey passed away in 2018, her family wanted to keep her vibrant way of life flowing. This
movement encourages us to put on our Red Glasses and to *live boldly, love big and pass it on*
like Audrey did. Audrey *knew her purpose.* We encourage you to *go find yours* and then *live it*
with a *fearless spirit.*

We invite you to visit the RGM website and hope that when you do, you enjoy their story as
much as we have and feel moved to share it with others. (And grab red glasses of your own!)

You. Defined!

"
Dare to go within ...
to *Define* what you want ...
to show up as *YOU!*
"

Alyssa Kreutzfeldt

& brilliantly grounded wisdom by
Cyndi Lesher

Alyssa Kreutzfeldt tells relatable stories touching, among other things, on grit and what grounds you, gratitude for the small things, and trusting in opportunities for growth—possibly when you least expect them. She poses questions that ask you to dig deeper and define who you are and what you want. Your answers will help you live and lead with greater authenticity and intention.

—Michael Solberg, President & CEO, Bell Bank

You. *Defined!* is a thought-provoking and inspiring book. There is a refreshing honesty and vulnerability in the author's approach to helping the reader align their deepest aspirations with what is necessary to achieve them. The book is full of powerful stories and insightful exercises. Highly recommended.

—David McNally, Best-selling author of *Even Eagles Need a Push* and *Mark of An Eagle*

Congratulations on creating a very unique volume filled with inspiration, combined with reality. You have told your journey beautifully, distilled it to key concepts that everyone can understand, and then grounded it with testimony, making your message real. I love that it has sticky qualities that I will refer to and reflect on.

—Myrna Marofsky, Founder of Business Women's Circle and

Chapter Chair for Women Presidents' Organization

Metaphorically speaking, Alyssa walks alongside you as you begin a journey of authenticity that allows you to first define and then create a beautifully intentional YOU! Interwoven with probing questions that require tremendous introspection, and generously sprinkled with powerful quotes that deliver mounds of motivation, Alyssa masterfully inspires you to journal your best life . . . and then launch it!

—Jan Ballman, Principal at Paradigm Reporting & Captioning, a Veritext Company

You. *Defined!*

Library of Congress Control Number: 2020901342
ISBN: 978-1-946195-63-0

Design by Michael Wasowicz
Copy Editing by Ellen Brill and Susan Olson

People become motivated when you guide them to the source of their own power. —Anita Roddick

Table of Contents

Howard Feiertag	*Robin Kocina*	*Steve Willock*	*Rob Amundson*
Camille Thomas	*John Jensvold*	*Patsy Levang*	*Rick S*
Shelly Meighan	*Ursula Pottinga*	*Laurie Stewart*	*Crystal Knotek*
Rod Axtell	*Michael Varney*	*Jennifer Smith*	*Randy Kroll*
Amy Jeatran	*Roger Gjellstad*	*Debb Klingel*	*Jeri Meola*
Jane Salmen	*Dick Bjorklund*	*Kim Plahn*	*Carey Lindeman*
Michael Geis	*Maureen Bausch*	*Jennifer Sayre*	

Meet the *Authors*

About Alyssa Kreutzfeldt…

Alyssa is a wife to Fred and mom to two priority blessings named Owen and Averee. She is the Founder of bar 33 leadership and Author of You. *Defined.* Alyssa is a certified Leadership Coach and Speaker, an Executive Director for the John Maxwell team, and a certified DISC personality profile Consultant.

To those who know her best, Alyssa is known as: genuine, savvy, and intentionally thoughtful; a leader who is *wildly passionate* about enlarging people from the inside-out.

For over two decades, Alyssa held a variety of key leadership roles in corporate America, as well as in numerous charitable and business organizations. She has been recognized as a top leader in business by the Minneapolis-St. Paul Business Journal, Minnesota Business, and National Association of Women Business Owners.

In December of 2015, she packaged her years of experience and launched bar 33 leadership – a leadership firm named after her family's cattle ranch in western North Dakota. *"Growing up on our ranch, I quickly learned that our brand was a genuine portrayal of our family and the inner nature of who we truly are. All of us had a profound commitment to do things right from the ground up."* Her devotion to become a lifelong student and ambassador of leadership and human potential was inspired by her family's deep-rooted values, character, and daily principles.

From personal experience, Alyssa knows that *who you are on the inside, is how you lead, live, and influence.* Through her speaking and coaching engagements, she guides people to boldly define their inner game and empowers them to be that - as an individual and as a leader. She'll leave you with an audacious inner fire that propels you to: *"Intentionally Own It!"*

Connect with Alyssa, on a weekly basis, for encouragement, positive belief, and inside-out growth. Find her inspiration at www.bar33leadership.com. *While on her site, check out the bar 33 leadership school for additional growth resources – including an online You. Defined! experience.*

Throughout the guided thinking section of this book, you'll find insight titled "Brilliantly Grounded Wisdom" prepared by Cyndi Lesher. Cyndi's wisdom is rooted in what she has experienced, observed, and chosen to learn throughout her years of life thus far.

About Cyndi Lescher . . . a work in progress, enjoying and appreciating this age and stage of life. Cyndi is retired from the corporate world, having held several leadership positions, including CEO of an energy company.

Cyndi is a community builder, philanthropist, people connector, non-profit volunteer, and is active in civic and church work. Cyndi serves on several non-profit boards, allowing her to utilize her head and heart to serve organizations and people about which she is passionate. She is a frequent speaker on leadership, effective communication, philanthropy, and realizing one's potential.

Cyndi credits her family and faith with providing her the grounded values, positive outlook, and resilience that is core to her life. She is a wife, mother, grandmother, and loyal friend. By far, the best title she has ever had is that of "Nana."

"When we choose to enlarge ourselves, we are equipped to enlarge the people around us: leadership is about the people, not the person."

"You can design and create and build the most wonderful place in the world. But it takes people to make the dream a reality." —Walt Disney

The 3 *G's:*
Grit, Gratitude & Growth

A span of life is nothing. But the man or woman who lives that span, they are something. They can fill that tiny span with meaning, so its quality is immeasurable, though its quantity may be insignificant. —Chaim Potok

Years back when I first met my husband, I asked him, "What do you do?"

"I'm a hand model," he replied.

His witty response made me laugh, yet his statement made me think, "What do our hands represent in each of our lives?"

Now, we actually may not be hand models, but our hands help us shape and define the direction of our lives. They reflect our choices and draft a story that someday will be the legacy of our life and leadership—In our homes, our community, and our places of work. They "do" what our head and heart has led them to pursue.

As children, one of the first things we learned to do is trace our hands. We made them into artwork like turkey hands, praying hands, and the kissing hand, just to name a few. We've also paid attention to how they grow, placing them up to another person to see whose is larger. "Mine is almost as big as yours," we would exclaim!

When a child is born, we wrap our hand around their little fist to express connection. When people are ill or nearing death, it's our hands that connect our hearts without exchanging a word.

I recall when we had to move my grandma from her home of many years to a nursing home. It was sudden, and she was not prepared for the moment; her eyes were filled with confusion, fear, and sadness. We gently grabbed her hand to assure her of our love and that everything would be okay. Without a word being exchanged, she felt the connection.

Our hands connect us to our hearts.
They connect us with our inner selves.
They connect us with those who we love.
They connect us with our life story—from birth to death.

Look at your hands . . .

What do they represent and what do you want them to represent in your lifetime?
What story have they written thus far?
What stories do you want them to continue to write and not write?
What do you want them to accomplish, work for, create, develop, and lead?
What untapped potential do they still need to chase?
How do you want them to handle the ups and downs of life?
How will they express love and compassion?
With what kindness will they be involved?

As you ponder these questions, and the many more that come to you, be mindful that how you influence your hands is within your control.

Your greatest message will be spoken by your life, not your lips. —Steven Furtick

When we choose to intentionally design our own story, we place ourselves in it and own it.

A few years back, my dad was heading to his fifty-year class reunion. Before leaving the house, I asked him, "What are you most looking forward to?" He shared that it was important to him to ask his classmates, "Has your life turned out the way you pictured it would when we left high school and had the whole world ahead of us?"

What a powerful question!

We only get answers to the questions we are brave enough to ask ourselves and wholeheartedly answer. Reflective questions allow us to think. To grow. To make edits. To lean in with intent.

Let's ask ourselves the same question, "Are you living the life you pictured you'd be living?"

Everyone loves a good story. Stories tell us who we are. Stories are us. —John Maxwell

Each day, when I look at my hands, I am reminded that it's up to me to direct how I use them. It's my choice to be intentional about the story I am allowing them to write and to recognize that my choices impact not only my life, but the lives of the many others I influence each day.

Have you thought about what your life will represent and what your life story will involve? *How will you fill the pages of your life to make your story great?*

When I think about what has influenced me to write the story I am in, the decisions and choices I've made thus far come to mind:

> What I've allowed to enter my life and what I have not.
> The risks I was willing to take and the ones I was not.
> The people with whom I have chosen to spend my time and those I have not.
> The opportunities in which I placed myself and the ones I did not.

Big or small, every decision and choice has shaped my path and the tone of my story.

For me, many (not all) of these choices aligned with what I value and the picture I had drawn for my life.

As my life moved ahead, somewhere along the line, parts of the story I was allowing my hands to write no longer felt like mine—the lines were getting a little blurry. I knew I needed to face it, yet digging deep to figure it out was something I was not willing to do. Quite honestly, it overwhelmed me, since I knew I would be forced to open my eyes differently and make changes.

As I kept negotiating "not now" with my inner nudge, I clung to all the "valid" reasons why I could ignore it, UNTIL I no longer could. The nudge from within got so intense that I had to face it.

At that moment, I chose to look up, to listen, and to make changes in the design of my professional and personal path. I made a commitment to face what wasn't working and to "reclaim me." I had allowed busyness, comfort, fear, and other people's ideas to hijack my life.

The story I was writing was no longer lining up with where I should be. I was off track and needed to be brave enough to allow my hands to start writing different chapters in my life story. I wasn't in a bad story—just no longer mine.

I had given someone else my pen, and I needed it back!

Don't let what you're afraid of keep you from what you were made for. —Bob Goff

At age 16 I was part of the state Student Council leadership conference in Bismarck, North Dakota. We sat on a cold, hard, gray floor while a speaker named Laurie Stewart engaged us in personal growth exercises. It was then that something deep within me clicked. I knew at that moment I would be "her" someday. I loved what she sparked in me, and I wanted to do the same for other leaders.

When we adjourned and went back to our lives, I wrote her a note. Her reply has been tucked into my vision journal, stamped with a clear and vivid personal promise: At age 40 I would start my own speaking and coaching business that would guide others to their inner brilliance, whatever that might look like for them.

For the next couple of decades, I continued to be a student of leadership and human potential. I studied, read, and exposed myself to opportunities that would grow and shape me, that would fill my toolbox with world-class resources I could bring to others.

I purposefully observed leadership styles, held leadership roles, and made mental notes along the way of what good leadership really is. I made certain that when 40 came, I was prepared for the launch of my dream!

With this dream in mind, I took the pen back and designed my "rock star plan."

I wrote it. I reviewed it. I had it!

It was clear. It had focus. It was lined with everything needed to "reclaim me. "

I WAS READY!

The first step was to make edits to my professional life. I jumped out of comfort into the unknown. Invigorated by boldness and driven by passion, I launched my dream business.

The initial jump felt right. As I entered the next jump and the next jump and the next, I started feeling uncertain and a bit fuzzy. I found myself doubting my plan and myself.

I had a handful of clients that I truly appreciated, yet something was off.

I had never fully experienced this before. I had seen this "look" in the eyes of the people I had guided and coached, yet I didn't truly know what the fear behind their look felt like.

I found myself thinking, "Wow, my dream didn't look or feel like this." THIS was not part of my rock star plan.

Although I had been in many conversations about how hard it is to move dreams forward, they were simply words—ones I heard yet never absorbed because I hadn't walked the path myself.

John Maxwell has shared, "The dream is always free; it's the journey that costs you." Anyone can dream and anyone can climb for a while. When it gets hard is when you start paying the price for your dream.

The journey of my dream was starting to get hard. It forced me to lean in—listen, refine, and move.

Another reality that slapped me in the face was the sense of loneliness.

I knew I was taking a step back to step forward, yet I had never walked this path before, and there were many things I found myself missing: daily interactions with a lot of people, a robust momentum that kept me stimulated and on my toes, partnering with my husband to make good money for our family and feeling that sense of accomplishment, thought partners to stimulate my thinking, adding value and joy to the daily lives of others, having a lot of people with whom to share my smile! (*I know this one may make you say, "What?"—yet it's real. Smiling at people throughout your day lifts who you are in an important way.*)

THIS sense of loneliness was not part of my plan either.

As I coached myself through the unexpected roller coaster of emotions, fuzziness, and mindset hurdles, a sudden shift happened. I was diagnosed with cancer.

When I learned the length and scope of the treatment ahead, I found myself flipped upside down both professionally and personally. It blew my mind that I was being placed on the sidelines of life, absolutely opposite where I placed myself in my "reclaiming me" rock star plan (and opposite of how I had lived life up to that moment!).

After I had a few moments to digest my reality, I pulled myself together and knew it was up to me to determine how I would allow my hands to write this part of my life story. It was my choice to find purpose in this pause and to view my sideline experience as an opportunity to grow. It was my choice to choose what mindset and perspective to take.

I chose to write this chapter as: The *3 G's:* Grit, Gratitude, & Growth

Here's why . . .

Life comes with lemons, yet we don't have to suck on them. —Max Lucado

I had an opportunity in front of me to focus on my vision, not my circumstances. I had an opportunity to shape the view of resiliency and vulnerability for myself, my kids, and perhaps others who were watching. I had an opportunity to make my mind work for me, not against me.

When I was able to shift my thinking and live above my circumstances, I began to see the meaning of this unexpected shift of season. Rather than being frustrated by the edits to my plan, I paused.

The word that I continued to notice was "within." I knew wholeheartedly that I had everything inside of me to navigate through this chapter—my internal anchors would be my guide. Yet, for me to be guided by them, I needed to fully know them, to remind myself of what they were since I hadn't needed to exercise them completely in a while. This was a moment of real and raw growth.

Create a life that feels good on the inside, not just one that looks good on the outside.

For over fifteen years of my life, I had been reading and studying about the power of our minds and how they literally direct every part of our body, including our performance and potential.

Our thinking, words, and emotions determine our proximity to our vision, goals, and people. I was fascinated with everything I was learning and tried to apply it to my own life, as well as use my knowledge to lift others.

When I started digging into my internal anchors to guide my hands in writing this "sidelines" chapter of life, I soon realized I was being tested. It's one thing to know how to keep your thoughts and mind working for you when life is life, but how do you do it when life is not going your way at all?

That's when I knew that I was being taken on a journey titled the *3 G's* and that what I would learn on that journey would equip me with grounded confidence, character, and courage. In order to gain it, *I* had to do the work—no one else could do it for me, nor would I want the pen in someone else's hand.

Now, looking back at my "rock star plan," it was about reclaiming me in God's vision, not mine. This unexpected time on the sidelines of life shaped the vision for my future in a way that allowed me to put my life and priorities into perspective and alignment, to grasp onto what's important, to dig deeper, to listen, and to get completely uncomfortable in order to be refined in ways necessary for my growth.

I let my heart, head, and hands sync as one (without trying to control every move)!

Here are the lessons behind each *G*. . .

Grit:

When you look up the definition of Grit, you'll find: Courage. Resolve. Strength of character and will. Moral fiber. Determination despite difficulties.

Until mid-2015, adversity was never really part of my life. Yes, I had moments for sure, yet nothing where I had to dig to the deepest part of my inner core to move forward in a productive fashion.

When my professional and personal life were flipped upside down at the same time, I had an opportunity to be lifted and guided by what grounds me. Those internal anchors gave me strength, dignity, clarity, and focus. They reminded me of how to show up, even during one of the hardest seasons in my life.

Haphak: A Hebrew word from the Old Testament for a turning-point moment: "In that moment, he became something new."

In this season, I chose to become something new.

Have you experienced a turning-point moment, or are you in that type of season right now? If so, did you allow, or are you allowing, it to intentionally shape you? What would move you to look at it from this lens?

> *Each transition to a new phase of purpose is accompanied by a crisis of uncertainty, a chaotic period of time in which we are organizing ourselves.*
>
> -Richard Leider

As I was forced to walk slowly through this chapter of life—a chapter that I wanted to sprint through because I don't like slow. But the slow and steady walk taught me a few lasting lessons. When I stopped trying to control the pace, a beautiful calm hit me. That's when I was able to go within and learn the meaning of the word "truly."

In that moment, I learned to truly . . .

> breathe, believe, and simply be;
> wholeheartedly place my trust in God;
> forgive myself and others;
> observe, absorb, and learn (and not just the nuggets I wanted to absorb);
> remain completely uncomfortable, trusting that it's leading me to greater growth.

The lesson: Once I embraced this "truly" stage, I was able to pause and reflect, giving myself the gift to think and listen from within. This allowed me to lean into the lessons this chapter was intended to bring to my life and to the lives of others—not to rush past them.

If the path you are on doesn't lead you deeper into yourself, it's not the right path.
—Lalah Delia

Gratitude

Have you ever played Tic Tac Toe or Connect Four? If so, have you noticed that when you focus on your next move and fail to look at what your partner is doing, you always lose?

Your perspective becomes so inward and narrow that you forget to look up.

As part of this journey, I was nudged to look up and not get self-consumed. What was placed on my heart was this: Look up. Notice. Act.

While on the sidelines, I was so absorbed in my health and focused on my professional life not coming together like I pictured it, that I failed to recognize all the good and all the prayers that *had* been answered. I wasn't noticing them because I was focusing inward . . . on "me."

When I learned to stop being consumed by "me," I thought about my life and realized it's not about me!! Nobody will really remember anything about me except the imprint I choose to make on them.

Naturally, we are all wired to be selfish—to think, "What about me?" To change that, I chose to look outward—to be intentional about noticing the good, to recognize all the blessings smothering me. I had to choose to look up, to notice, to act.

I still remember the days that I once prayed for what I have now.

I have been told that both you and I will see around 25,000 images in a day, that our reticular activation system are the eyes of our brain. We can choose to condition our eyes (like athletes who watch tape after tape of another team to see where the opportunities are) to see the blessings in our lives and look for opportunities to be a blessing to others.

When we intentionally look up, notice, and act, we are given the opportunity to be necessary to someone—to be their blessing, to be their daymaker. When we choose to live our lives from that lens, we become bigger on the inside, which makes us better on the outside.

Being intentionally grateful shapes our perspective in a powerful way. We condition our eyes to see the good because that's what we're looking for. We train our minds to know that each day good things will happen to us and good things will happen through us. Big and small, we intentionally notice them.

Gratitude keeps us focused on the present and makes us happy. —Max Lucado

If you choose to purposefully train your mind to embrace this way of thinking, I promise you, it's the most refreshing way to view life! It will place a smile in your heart and guide you to naturally shape your thoughts to notice the good around you, anticipate you will find it, and develop a positive mental attitude.

It does not make you naïve or soft; it simply means you are choosing to shift your perspective and focus. When you intentionally choose this shift, you'll bring enormous blessings to others and abundance to your world too.

The lesson: Look up. Notice. Act.

Growth

It was up to me to use the sidelines as an opportunity to grow, to be intentional about choosing growth.

Growth is a silent investment—it does not speak up, it shows up. —John Maxwell

As I already shared, this shift was not fitting in my vision, instead, what I learned is that my sidelines experience allowed me to put my life and priorities into perspective and to be reminded of what they truly are. It allowed me to get completely uncomfortable so I could expand in a healthy way.

John Maxwell teaches, "You can't bring people to places you have never been." If I have never *really* faced adversity or the opportunity to be resilient, how could I lead others through the wilderness successfully?

We will all have wilderness moments, and if we don't have the critical skills to navigate through them, we'll get stuck.

While on my cancer journey, losing my hair was a scary step for me. I know it may sound vain, and it probably is, yet it was a real fear. I did not want to look the part of cancer. Once I did, I would no longer be able to mask or pretend as if something major was not occurring in my life.

Although it was difficult, it was truly one of the biggest growth moments in my life.

When I removed my wig and started to let the world into my journey on a different level, I had a friend ask me, "Do you feel beautiful?" That question stopped me. When I reflected on it, I landed confidently on the answer, "Yes, and it's different."

Although my appearance had dramatically changed, my heart, mind, and soul had not. They actually had been strengthened and enhanced. That "within" piece God was talking to me about is what moved me forward; it placed a smile on my face and helped others feel comfortable when they didn't know what to say.

Choosing to grow from the inside out allowed me to walk into a hockey rink that a year before, I had thought to myself, "There is no way I will ever go out in public without my 'Alyssa look' of long blonde hair. I will not look like that lady across the foyer who has no hair, and she's still smiling and part of life. That will not be me."

Little did I know what was ahead. . . .

Fast forward a year, my husband and son had already left for the rink. When my daughter and I were almost ready, I went to grab my wig to throw it on. That's when I stopped, looked at myself in the mirror, and thought, "If not now, when?" At that moment I took a deep breath, set my wig aside, and grabbed some big earrings and my favorite lipstick. With my heart pounding, I thought, "I can do this."

When my daughter and I pulled up to the rink and began walking in, I casually looked up and suddenly stopped and just stared. When I looked at the rink entrance, it was the same one that one year (almost to the day) prior I told myself, "There is no way. . . ."

What I learned is that when we choose to embrace the difficulties and vulnerable moments in our lives through the lens of growth, we grow.

We grow in ways that make us authentically beautiful—no longer in a vain fashion, but in a fashion that is grounded and anchored from the inside.

We give others courage and permission to embrace their wilderness moments with confidence and character. *We become real, together. People crave real. We can relate to real. Vulnerability connects us.*

We all encounter stumbling blocks or stepping stones in life. It's our choice to turn them into moments of growth.

This shift in season brought me to my purpose—a more direct route to my dream.

When I drafted my "rock star" plan, it looked different—quite different. When my cancer journey brought me through many rounds of chemo and surgeries, I had a lot more time to think and reflect.

What I learned when my plan did not go as I imagined is, I need to trust—always—not just when life is comfortable and I can breathe. I learned to trust even when I feel like my chest is caving in, when absolutely nothing is going my way, and I feel tossed aside.

The lesson: Choose growth—no matter how uncomfortable it may be. Choose to ask yourself hard questions. Choose to think from within. Choose to be vulnerable. Choose to let the difficult chapters in life and leadership refine you in a purposeful fashion.

Imagine...

The world is but a canvas to the imagination. —Henry David Thoreau

When I reflect upon my *3 G's* chapter of Grit, Gratitude, & Growth, the word *imagine* comes to mind.

For a moment, think of the word imagine. . . . When we were younger, we were always imagining life.

Let yourself get into that mindset again. Remove the outside clutter, noise, and chaos, and let yourself think from the inside.

Imagine . . .

knowing who you are from the inside out and bringing that forward;

being grounded by your internal anchors;

reaching your potential in life;

believing in yourself and loving who you are;

thinking inward to confidently write a life story that is YOU. Truly you.

Imagine a resource that will help shape and design the picture of your life and leadership, a guide that will inspire you to see it, feel it, believe it. . . . *intentionally own it!*

This book will empower you to tap into your imagination. It's designed to be a tidy spot for you to land your thinking and log what you want to bring forward in life, to *believe* it will happen.

By intentionally building your emotional and intellectual core, you'll be able to navigate through different phases of life (both the highs and the lows) in a grounded state of mind. In a manner that anchors your resilience from within.

When we get out of touch with our core, we lose our life perspective.

Years back when I worked at the Minneapolis Chamber of Commerce, a luncheon speaker shared a statement that stuck with me: "Many of us are too busy to be successful."

You can choose to find the time to get better—to pause, to think, to reflect, to determine if what is in your life should be there—if how you're showing up, in all circles, is a genuine reflection of who you are. Or you can choose "busy."

Often we are "too busy" to intentionally pause and ask ourselves reflective questions because the answers to our questions are perhaps ones we don't want to face, yet we know we must. Or perhaps the sense of busyness makes us feel important. I know I was there. . . .

A while ago my mom would say to me often, "Alyssa, you are too corporate."

I didn't stop to ask her what she meant by that statement (because I didn't want the answer) until I knew I had to.

My husband and I were at a large, prestigious fundraising gala with which I had been deeply involved, and a gentleman at our table said, "It must be amazing to be married to her." And my husband's response to him was, "Try it."

It caught both of us off guard, yet his frustration was real. My mom's words were real.

My personal definition of success wasn't aligning with the impact I wanted to make. I was giving my best to others and had very little left for my family—or even for me.

I was not reflective, I was busy—really, really busy. I was capturing a lot of professional recognition, yet was this what I wanted? Who was winning? Were my motives pure? I certainly looked "successful" in the eyes of others, yet was it lining up with my personal picture of success?

In one part of my career, I recall sitting at an awards luncheon where I was the recipient of The Real Power 50 award and, a month later, the Top 25 Women in Business. I sat at the table thinking, "Is this all worth it?" Is how I am showing up at home a reflection of the recognition I am walking on the stage to capture? Am I being true to what I value?

I was the only one who could pause and ask myself some raw questions and answer them in a whole-hearted fashion—not just for me, but for those who experienced me.

When I truly stopped to reflect and ask myself questions that penetrated deep thinking, I had some adjustments to make. What was real and true to me was off track. What those closest to me were experiencing did not match what I valued or pictured as true leadership, happiness, or success.

Yes, all the recognition felt good, yet those *in* my world needed me to show up differently.

I needed to get back to my core and exercise it differently. The *foundation of coaching* is where I found my realignment and answers.

Dare to Go Within

The gate to successful living opens inward. Pushing gets you nowhere. —Edward Kramer

We are programmed naturally to think from the outside in. Often we try to make changes from the outside, yet our answers can't be found somewhere outside of us; they are always within us. We must learn to think and to live from the inside out.

It's not more knowledge, data, and information that we need—it's self-awareness. Choices are a function of our awareness. We uncover this side of us when we choose intentionally to pause and to ask ourselves searching questions, questions that allow us to define what's true for us—not what's true for someone else.

When we ask others for advice or the answer, we condition ourselves not to think. Thinking is the hardest work there is, yet it's the only way we become resourceful. It's how we bring clarity and focus to our own life in a bold and confident fashion. *(There is a big difference between mental activity and thinking. The quality of your life will be in direct proportion to the quality of the thinking you apply to it.)*

While becoming certified as a professional speaker and coach, I fell in love with the power of questions, questions that stimulate the type of thinking experience that makes the unconscious conscious—the type that brings people around to their own truth, and from this foundation equips them with grounded confidence from the inside out.

We all have the answers within us, we simply are not conscious of them yet. Specific types of searching questions get us there. That's what I fell in love with and want to transfer to you.

The true process of coaching does not tell you what to think, it inspires *you to think.*

We can all "know" a lot of stuff, but that will not bring clarity to our lives or allow us to be resilient in phases that are stretching our core. In order to create lasting change, we must adopt a learning approach from the inside out. Coaching is the most powerful form of behavior transformation.

There are three underlying objectives to coaching:

1) Self- discovery

2) Self-awareness

3) Choices

Coaching is proactive. It takes you from where you are today to where you intend to be in the future. It empowers you to understand and adopt your own truths. Equipping you to take complete responsibility and accountability for your life, it brings clarity to your choices.

You will never self-actualize in this lifetime, if you fail to go within. —Christian Simpson

Are you ready to be the coach of your life? To ask yourself questions that allow you to land at answers that are true for you?

When I was in middle school, my parents had my sister and me participate in 4-H livestock judging. I often reflect on our experience and appreciate what I gained from it.

Prepare yourself:

We were expected to do our pre-work and study the livestock breeds so once we arrived at each meet, we were prepared for what was ahead.

Believe in your inner knowledge:

While in session, I learned to observe each class; to think; to ask myself questions about what I was seeing; to form my own individual thoughts; to transfer my beliefs to a panel of judges in an organized, confident, and succinct fashion.

We were not allowed to capture insight or suggestions from anyone else—we had to go within for our answers and believe, not question ourselves.

How this pertains to life . . . When I take time to think—to form *my own* ideas and thoughts; to move forward in life with *my* originality, not someone else's—I win and so does everyone else around me. (Just like I did in livestock judging; I took state!)

When I intentionally chose to believe in myself and not cloud my thoughts with the perspective, opinions, or ideas of others, I became inwardly resourceful, which fostered grounded confidence and clarity.

That's my passion for you! To inspire you to consciously participate in your life—to cut through the internal and external chaos, clutter, and noise, allowing you to become clear on what *you* most want for your life and leadership.

Ground *Rules*

We're almost ready to dive into the guide, but before we do, here's a few *ground rules*:

Uncomfortable is a gift!

Our greatest growth happens outside of our comfort zone, yet we are often taught to think from within it. Most people will surrender what they want for what is comfortable, familiar, and safe. You must come to terms with being outside of your comfort zone to grow!

Look forward!

We often look to our past or current situation to see if there is any evidence that where we want to go is possible. We're looking in the wrong direction—the resources are inward.

Think, yet don't over-think!

As you walk through this book, remember there are no right or wrong answers, but there are answers that are true for you. Boldly set your intentions!

Remove the limits!

Many of us are living limiting lives. Be who you want to be. Release your own limited concept of yourself. Believe in the intentions you set for each section, and move toward them boldly. *DO NOT* come into agreement with any of your limiting beliefs!

Have fun!

As John Maxwell states, "You can live life however you want, yet you only get one life to live." Make it yours! *Intentionally* own it!

I don't fear failure. I fear succeeding at something that does not matter. —Dan Erickson

Define What You Want

Your mind must arrive at your destination before your life does.

Before launching into the self-coaching portion of this guide, there is one major topic that needs to be understood and embraced in order to allow this book to work for you.

This guide is intended to be BOTH a tidy and organized spot for you to land your thinking AND a resource that allows you to feel, see, and know that what you are writing for each section you *believe* to be true for you.

Almost every great book about human potential starts out with *mindset*. The mind is the epicenter of performance. Everything is an expression of our mind.

Whether we are aware of it or not, we're in charge of our own mind; we're creating our results from moment to moment.

In the 1950s Edward Kramer wrote a book titled, *Pathways to Power*. In this book he teaches the topic of synchromantics, known as the science of life balance.

Synchromantics is simply taking you from where you are to where you want to be— synchronizing your *desired objective* with your *physical action* until they are in balance.

We can spend our time listening to great instruction, thinking into each section, defining what we know to be true and original to our personal picture of life and leadership, yet, if we fail to link it to what we *believe* will happen, the picture for each section will simply remain as words with no forward momentum.

Make sense?

There is nothing new about this. We all use it, whether you know it or not. It's how we accomplish whatever we do well.

Invite your inward eyes and inward ears to define what you most want in life. As Edward Kramer has shared, "Point to your heart, not your head, for ideas and answers. We live out of our hearts."

Law of Living: Letting go of the outer world and daring to listen to the voice within.

Thinking is the map. Action is the journey. Feeling is the answer. —Edward Kramer

Thinking is the map . . .

For each section of this guide, determine your core objective by asking yourself:

What is it that you most want?

Why is that? What makes you want this?

What will be the result of you getting it? What will it do for you?

Action is the journey . . .

Whatever you want most, assume with the *heart of you,* the *feeling of you,* that it is already yours. For example, what would be the physical attitude that you would have if you already had what you wanted?

When you discover that answer, take on that tone, pace, energy level, smile, relaxed spirit, speech, confidence, etc., until it becomes automatic.

Feeling is the answer . . .

According to Edward Kramer, our end objective is always a "sense of" feeling—security, satisfaction, belonging, accomplishment, fulfillment, possession, love, or joy.

Connecting what you most want to the feeling is important. What you *feel* to be true is what you experience.

Action and feelings always go together; they act as one and are in perfect balance.

We can't depend on our intellect to reach our goal of satisfaction, because it does not recognize the way you feel. That's why we point to our heart for answers and ideas.

The longest distance in the world is between the head and the heart. When we move from our head to our heart, that's when we become invested. —Michael J. Formica

Clarity is the most important concept in establishing and living an organized life. —John Maxwell

A soundtrack that captured my attention is from the movie, *The Greatest Showman*. The lyrics to some of the songs move us to be brave and inspire us to live in a world that *we* design.

With that frame of mind, it's time to ask again, *"Are you ready to ask yourself questions that inspire you to consciously participate in your life, questions that allow you to become clear on what you want your life and leadership to be about?"*

Each section of this guide is designed to stimulate thinking that's *yours.* There are many pages of white space for you to land your thinking and own what is true for you.

Similar to my livestock judging days, *you* are the only one that can observe, think, and allow your hands to design, for each section, a truth that is *authentically* yours!

Get your *head to think it,* your *heart to feel it,* your *hands to move it* into action!

Begin with the answer within you . . . to begin at any other point is to work away from the answer. —Edward Kramer

One last foundational thought before we dive in: While listening to a message by Richard Leider, the author and speaker of *The Power of Purpose,* I was struck by something. What he shared resonated with me, as it sets the stage for the work ahead of you in the pages to come.

Richard has spent over thirty years uncovering the topic of purpose. As part of his research and writing, every few years he interviews people over the age of 65 (all over the world) and asks this question: "If you could do your life over again, what would you do differently?"

He has found three common themes that come from this question. People would:

1. Be more reflective the second time around. They would take a step back and look at the big picture.
2. Take more risks—not the risks of climbing mountains or kayaking rivers, but the risks of authenticity and voice. They would bring more of themselves into the equation of their life.
3. Discern their own bottom line, to determine for themselves what really matters. Every human being wants their life to matter. It does not have to be a big thing, yet it must feel real and authentic to them.

Show Up as *YOU!*

Making a wholehearted commitment to being happy is powerful medicine. —Robert Holden

This book was written with YOU in mind. It has been purposely crafted to help you consciously participate in your life—to cut through the internal and external chaos, clutter, and noise . . . to *Dar*e to go within . . .to *Define* what you want . . . to show up as *YOU!*

Throughout our combined years of leadership experience and focus on intentional growth, Cyndi and I have noticed a theme of categories that, when defined, anchor a person from the inside out.

It is our sincere hope that this book sparks an inside out connection for you, in a fashion that's *original* and *authentic* to who you are—inspiring you to **own** *your true brand of brilliance!*

Here's the flow:

> *Step One:* Each section will have a category title. Allow yourself to absorb it; think into it; imagine it.
>
> *Step Two:* The heartbeat of this book is in the questions that line each section. They were designed to help you go within for the answer. Take on that mindset and marinate in each one; let your answers come to you. Don't doubt them!
>
> *Step Three:* Use the white space on the pages titled, "*Define* what you want," to take what's rumbling inside you, then write out in detail what's real and true to you.
>
> *Step Four:* Make it real. Make it happen. *Intentionally* own it!

Let's get started!!!

Have the courage to live life the way you want to. —Brene Brown

You. Defined!

"
Dare to go within ...
to Define what you want ...
to show up as YOU!
"

Define your picture of *Intentionality.*

People who embrace intentional living move from a life of observation, good intentions, and wishing, into a life of action and doing. They are committed.

In his book *Intentional Living*, John Maxwell shares that when you choose to live intentionally, you will: Re-affirm your values; find your voice; develop your character and experience inner fulfillment.

In what ways are you living a life that's intentional and true to who you are?

What inspires you to be intentional in those areas?

In which area(s) of life must you become more intentional?

When you do, what will this do for you?

What would hold you back from becoming more intentional in these key areas?

When you think of what you value, how committed are you to being intentional in these areas of your life?

What will help you become more intentional and committed in these priority areas?

One a scale of one to ten, how committed are you to developing your ability to grow—in the areas of awareness, character, choices, etc.? What will inspire you to expand as a person?

Anything else?

Intentionally own it!

What is one discipline you must be consistently committed to today and every day, in order to succeed at living with intention?

When you do this, what will this mean to you?

Intentionality

[Brilliantly Grounded Wisdom prepared by Cyndi Lesher]

My life experiences have been, like most people, a mix of joy, sorrow, ordinary, and extraordinary. And, like most people, *life gets messy, and it's easy to get caught up in the busyness and the allure of bright, shiny objects.*

I started *paying attention to what I needed instead of what I wanted.* That has made all the difference for me. I'm able to focus on my true needs and look for the life lessons to which I need to pay attention.

These lessons have provided me *the gift of clarity.* I can see clearly now.

Ask yourself, *"Are you living a filled-full life or a fulfilled life?"* What may need to shift to ensure it's a fulfilled life?

_____

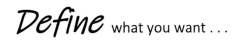

Define what you want . . .

When you're intentional, you can add value to everything you do and to every person you meet. —John Maxwell

*Define* what you want . . .

Don't let the noise of others' opinions drown out your inner voice. —Steve Jobs

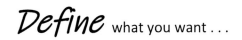 *Define* what you want . . .

Consult not your fears but your hopes and your dreams. Think not about your frustrations, but about your unfulfilled potential. Concern yourself not with what you tried and failed in, but with what is still possible for you to do. —Pope John XXIII

 *Define* what you want . . .

True belonging is not something we achieve, accomplish, or negotiate with others, it's something we carry in our hearts. Our wild, messy heart. —Brene Brown

Define your picture of *Potential.*

It is a shocking fact that everybody's idea of themselves is far below their capabilities.

In John Maxwell's book *No Limits*, he shares the **Capacity Challenge**: If you grow in your **awareness**, develop your **abilities**, and make the right **choices**, you can reach your **capacity**. *(Most people use only 10 percent of their true potential.)*

Describe what you believe about your potential.

How closely does that picture align with your reality?

What does this picture of potential mean to you?

Who would you like to be, and what would you like to do?

What are you doing to realize your potential?

Describe the changes you need to make to become all you can be. What do you need to give up so that you can dedicate yourself to excellence?

Is there anything getting in the way or affecting your ability to reach your true potential capacity (e.g., mindset, self-image, trust, fear, desire, chaos, other)?

What steps, both today and in the future, can you take to improve that?

What do you need to start doing today to move into what you know you're capable of? When you do, what will this do for you?

Anything else?

Intentionally own it!

What is your overall plan for personal growth?

What are specific things you will do every day to bring it to reality? What will it take to commit yourself to following through on it consistently?

Potential

[Brilliantly Grounded Wisdom prepared by Cyndi Lesher]

If we did all the things we were capable of doing, we would literally astound ourselves.
—Thomas A. Edison

Remember when you were young, in high school, and your parents and teachers kept telling you to "live up to your potential? "

For me, this theme continued in college, and my advisor told me, "Cyndi, you're not living up to your potential." It was so frustrating to me because I thought I was doing all the right stuff—studying hard, making good grades, getting involved in organizations, and assuming leadership positions when asked. I was living up to my potential. What did people expect of me anyway?

Once again, when I was going into my junior year in college, my advisor said to me "Cyndi, I don't think you are living up to your potential."

I snapped back, "Well, what is my potential and what more does everyone expect of me!?"

Professor McNurlen smiled and replied, "Ah-hah, you see *you are living up to everyone else's expectations but not your own. Think about what you want, your passions, and how you want to spend your life. Then you will define your potential based on what you think, need, and want to contribute to the world."*

Wow! That was truly a life-changing moment for me.

It was the *first time I spent time reflecting on me*—what I wanted for myself—*not what other people thought I should be or do.*

When Professor McNurlen pushed me to realize my potential, the rest fell in place.

When I was in the last semester of my senior year, he wrote my parents a letter telling them what a joy it had been to advise me and see me figure out my potential and reach it. He changed my life, and he was thanking me!

Eyes on the prize as they say. Professor McNurlen helped me see what is possible—what my potential was.

As we let our light shine, we unconsciously give other people permission to do the same.
—Nelson Mandela

P.S. Thank you, Dr. McNurlen!

*Define* what you want . . .

The strongest force in the human personality is the need to stay consistent with how we define ourselves. —Tony Robbins

 *Define* what you want . . .

I know who I am beneath whatever I happen to be wearing. I'm confident about who that guy is—and isn't. —Chip Gaines

Define what you want . . .

There is no heavier burden than an unfulfilled potential. —Charles Shulz

Define what you want . . .

At the end of the day, at the end of the week, at the end of my life, I want to say I contributed more than I criticized. —Brene Brown

Define your *Life.*

We act in accordance with what is meaningful to us.

Our plans miscarry because they have no aim. When a person does not know what harbor he or she is making for, no wind is the right wind. —Lucius Annaeus Seneca

What is it that you plan to do with your life? What's your vision?

What is it that you most want out of life? What difference do you want to make? What type of person do you desire to be?

What makes this important to you?

What would keep you from making this picture come true? What needs to change to move past that obstacle?

What is your personal bottom line? Why are you doing what you are doing in your life? What are you trying to accomplish?

What will be the result of fulfilling your vision?

What area of your life cries out for change and why? What would you change about how you are currently living? What new things would you add in?

What are some of your personal barriers to change? How will you intentionally move through them?

What makes you love your life? If you're not in love with it, what will it take to change that?

If you could write your future story, what would it look like?

Anything else?

Intentionally own it!

What must you do to maximize the phase of life you are in today? Looking ahead at the next phase, what can you do better now to prepare for the future?

Life

[Brilliantly Grounded Wisdom prepared by Cyndi Lesher]

I couldn't have imagined saying this thirty years ago, but I'm saying it now: I love being 70 years old! Sure, I have aches and pains, and spandex is not my friend, but *grit and determination have shaped me* with a lot of experiences, joys, sorrows, victories, and just plain living, which gives me the *power of perspective.*

Perspective enables you to choose a life that matters to you, learn and apply life lessons, and develop resiliency—all of which are fundamental to a balanced and joyful life. Here are some of the things that have worked for me:

Decide to dance

"Honey, life can be a ballroom dance or it can be full of crap. Your job in both cases is to watch your step." —Jane's House of Curl

That's good and insightful advice. She is referring to *the power we have to position ourselves intentionally.*

It's about an attitude of gratitude and choosing power over powerlessness. If you can't find happiness along the way, you won't find it at the end of the road. So don't wait.

Be present

Instead of racing against the clock, slow down and pay attention to what you're experiencing while you're experiencing it. *Being intentional in the moment requires practice.*

I regret that it took me so long to develop this skill because I missed a lot of my life that I can't get back. For example, I would be in a meeting, thinking of the meeting I had just come from and the meeting I was going to. While at my kid's soccer game, I would be thinking about the meeting I had just come from and the dinner party I was having Saturday, and on it goes.

I was living my life in sound bites and snippets. No wonder I felt frustrated, anxious, and like it was never enough—because it wasn't.

When I retired, the transition to retirement was a lot harder than I had envisioned. I was *unprepared for the "emotional" impact.* It felt a little like experiencing identity theft for me—without a title WHO ARE YOU?

I regret that I did not *spend more time on who I was vs. what I did.*

The concept of positional power vs. personal power became very clear.

Spend time, as you go, on who you are and practice being present. It makes a tremendous difference in the quality of your life and relationships. Try it; practice it. You'll like it.

> Your life is happening now, are you present?
>
> What are you doing now for your self-development that expands your perspective?
>
> Who in your life can help you practice mindfulness/intentionality?

Define what you want . . .

It's always worth it to be the truest version of ourselves. —Lisa Jo Baker

Define what you want . . .

Whenever you stay true to yourself, whenever you rock it with confidence, whenever you choose to not doubt yourself, people gravitate to that. Live original! —Sadie Robertson

Define what you want . . .

No one can make you feel inferior without your consent. —Eleanor Roosevelt

Define what you want . . .

You are always responsible for how you act, no matter how you feel. Remember that! Nobody can force you to have a bad attitude if you don't want to. —John Maxwell

Define your picture of *Happiness.*

The secret to a good life may be as simple as one word: *Happiness.*

Happiness is a habit; it is a state of being, not becoming. It is the natural outcome of being aligned with our authentic self.

What is *your* personal picture of happiness?

How close does that picture look to your reality?

What would it take to laser in on that picture and make it real?

What does happiness mean to you and your results in life and business?

What do you intentionally blend into each day that fosters a happy attitude?

How does gratitude and kindness show up in your picture of happiness? What are you intentionally doing each day for others?

Is there anything you need to face that isn't working? Any changes you need to make? If so, in what ways are you holding yourself back from making them?

How are the relationships in your life affecting your overall picture of happiness?

What would your life look like if you chose to intentionally live in your picture of happiness?

Anything else?

Intentionally own it!

On a daily basis, in which ways can you make your own day by choosing to make your day better? What's one thing you can do each day to notice others and act on making their day better too?

Ask yourself, "What will I do today to create a positive ripple effect in the world around me?" *This* mindset is an inward choice!

Foster *Happy* in ALL you do!

Happiness

[Brilliantly Grounded Wisdom prepared by Cyndi Lesher]

On May 7, 2001, my younger sister committed suicide by overdosing on prescription drugs. I found her with her beloved dog lying by her side.

I was profoundly sad, traumatized, and grief-stricken. Many of the details I don't remember clearly, because the brain has a beautiful way of protecting itself from what you aren't able to handle, until you can.

What I vividly remember is the coroner saying to me, as they were taking my sister out in a body bag, "You are going to need to get help for this, because it is too hard to handle by yourself; life is just too hard for some people."

He was right, and I took his advice. I also started paying attention to the increase in teenage suicides and suicide in general. Within the past years two famous people committed suicide in the same week—Kate Spade and Anthony Bourdain. People paid attention because they had fame and wealth.

I've learned not to look but to *see* people and practice kindness and compassion.

Everyone you meet is fighting a battle you know nothing about. Be kind. Always. —Britt Hume

———————————————————

Define what you want . . .

People are just as happy as they make up their minds to be. —Abraham Lincoln

 *Define* what you want . . .

You can't be selfish and happy at the same time. —Joyce Meyer

*Define* what you want . . .

You have brains in your head; you have feet in your shoes; you can steer yourself any direction you choose. —Dr. Seuss

*Define* what you want . . .

Maybe the journey isn't so much about becoming anything. Maybe it's about unbecoming everything that really isn't you, so you can be who you were meant to be in the first place.
—Unknown

Define your picture of *Success.*

Research shows that many people rate success as the most-coveted result they want from their work and life.

Success is an inward job. It comes from who we are within ourselves and helps to shape our priorities and choices.

What is your personal definition of success? What does that picture really look like—not to the world but to you?

Describe your desire for success. What does it mean to you?

How has your picture of success changed throughout the years?

Who influences your definition of success?

What would need to occur for you to consider yourself successful?

On what goals do you want to spend your life pursuing?

A statement shared by John Maxwell is, *"Successful people are not always significant. But significant people are always successful."*

What does this statement mean to you?
What is your personal picture of significance? What makes it important to you?
What can you do to enhance this picture and shift from a mindset of success to significance?
What would make you embrace it?
What would hold you back or draw you away? Why is that?

Anything else?

Intentionally own it!

What's one daily habit you can adopt to ensure you notice and celebrate your daily wins?

Making this a priority will condition your mind to build upon your successes, not failures—fostering a positive mindset and giving energy to forward-thinking momentum.

Success

[Brilliantly Grounded Wisdom prepared by Cyndi Lesher]

A few years back I went to an early meeting, then met my friend for coffee. I ordered my coffee and was quite pleased when the barista said, "Thank you, Cyndi Lesher." I was feeling pretty good that she knew who I was.

As I sat down with my friend, who was waiting at the table for me, she said, "So, what's the deal with wearing a name tag that says, 'Hello—my name is Cyndi Lesher'?" I explained I had been to an early meeting and had forgotten to take it off. I had to laugh as my ego trip was quickly over.

The Lesson: *Beware of the puffed-up ego. God has a way of checking that.*

Define what you want . . .

Self-trust is the first secret of success. —Ralph Waldo Emerson

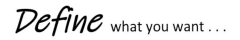

Define what you want . . .

Choose to be great at being present, great at being kind, and great at being you. —Unknown

Define what you want . . .

We cannot always choose what happens to us, but we can choose what happens in us.
—John Maxwell

Define what you want . . .

85 percent of your happiness and joy in life will be associated with your relationships. Always make them priority. —Brian Tracy

Define your guiding *Values & Principles.*

Values are essential to your life.

What you value and believe is the soul of who you are; it is your behavioral compass, your personal code of conduct. It defines how you show up and what you stand for.

As George H Lorrimer has stated, *"Back of every life there are principles that have fashioned it."* What are yours?

What do you stand for?

What are some of the core qualities that are true to you?

Who are you from the inside out?

What characteristics do you notice and value in others?

What must you have in your life to experience fulfillment?

What values are essential to supporting your inner self?

What guiding principles anchor who you are and determine how you show up, no matter the situation?

What can you do to simplify yourself by aligning your values and priorities?

What's showing up in your life that does not align with your values?

Where do you start when it comes to living life according to your values?

Anything else?

Intentionally own it!

What's one thing you can do to ensure your values align with what you say "yes" and "no" to in life?

Values & Principles

[Brilliantly Grounded Wisdom prepared by Cyndi Lesher]

My experience my whole adult life has affirmed for me that *behavior is not sustainable without values. Understand that character comes before personality. You must have character underneath to support it.* Without it, you are a hollow, superficial person. When times get tough or you are put to the test, it's your values that matter and sustain you.

Know what you stand for, so when you are tested (and you will be) you will know what to do. Values provide you with clarity and confidence, and are a model of authentic personal and professional leadership. Here's what's worked for me:

Live out loud. Say what you think. Express yourself, your thoughts, your beliefs. *"It's better to be a lion for a day than a sheep for life."* —Sister Elizabeth Kenny

Be a person of substance and character and it will serve you well. People who age well and persevere through adversity share four attributes:

> *A sense of purpose* – That's your vision. Visions hold power and provide you a bigger picture focus, which is important. Most people don't do that until presented with a crisis. *Know what you stand for.*

> *A sense of a higher being/power* – That's your spiritual side, whatever that means to you—something bigger than yourself.

> *A future focus* – Look forward and do not get stuck in the past. Look forward with anticipation, not dread.

> *A sense of humor* – *Laughter produces endorphins and makes you feel better.* It's true.

Be gentle with yourself. *Don't be too structured or too strict with yourself.* "Think of all the people on the Titanic who passed up dessert at dinner that fateful night." —Erma Bombeck

Simplify your life. I had previously tried to simplify my life. But I finally figured out I had it wrong. *I needed to simplify myself.* That's why the constant struggle to try to balance and control the various aspects of my life didn't work. Simplify yourself, and the rest works.

Life isn't a straight line. People are most simply human. We all experience loss, tragedy, and sorrow. That's why it is so important to develop supportive relationships, trusted friends, and a spiritual community.

Ask for help when you need it. *It's a sign of strength, not weakness.* Reach out when you need to. During an interview with Buzz Aldrin, the astronaut, he was asked about how challenging, courageous, and scary it must have been to go to the moon. He replied, "Going to the moon was easy," then revealed that his mother and sister had both committed suicide.

Life is not a straight line.

━━━

*Define* what you want . . .

It's not hard to make decisions when you know what your values are. —Roy Disney

*Define* what you want . . .

We can't be "all in" if only parts of us show up. If we're not living, loving, or leading with our whole, integrated hearts, we're doing it only halfheartedly. You either walk inside your story and own it or you stand outside your story and hustle for your worthiness. —Brene Brown

 *Define* what you want . . .

Try not to become a man of success, but rather a man of value. —Albert Einstein

 *Define* what you want . . .

People can't live with change if there's not a changeless core inside of them. The key to change is a changeless sense of who you are, what you are about, and what you value.
—Stephen R. Covey

Define your *Priorities.*

Your success and fulfillment in life will depend on how well you fill the hours of your day. Nobody can manage time but we all can manage those things that take up our time.

Look at your calendar . . . does it reflect the life you want to have?

Describe how you have prioritized your life up until now. What do you need to do to improve that?

Review your schedule and to-do's. What dominates most days? Most weeks?

Are you filling each day with things you want to be doing in life?

In which ways are these activities serving your vision and values?

What are you spending time on that gives you the greatest return?

What must show up each day to make your life what you want it to be?

How do you determine what lands in your life/on your schedule and what does not?

When you look at your commitments . . .

Which parts are draining you dry? What do you dread?

Which ones need to be reconsidered?

Which ones must stay?

What can you do 5 percent more of, or 5 percent less of, to help you get to where you want to be?

Anything else?

Intentionally own it!

Make every day count. —Gary Voggesser

Each day think, "How will I *intentionally* make *this* day count?"

Priorities

[Brilliantly Grounded Wisdom prepared by Cyndi Lesher]

Years back, when I was growing in my corporate career my ultimate boss and CEO of the company gave me this advice, "*If you make a commitment, keep it.*"

I've practiced that advice over the years, and it has served me well, especially when I really came to understand what it means. *It means keeping a promise and defines the kind of person you are—one who shows up and can be counted on. It is a measure of your integrity and reliability.*

Recently, I was tempted to ignore that advice and blow off a meeting. I gave myself various excuses - I was tired; I had a headache; the traffic sucked...blah, blah, blah. But that little voice in the back of my head kept saying, "*if you make a commitment, keep it.*"

So, begrudgingly I went to the meeting.

Imagine my surprise when the meeting opened with recognition of the 2019 Trustee of the Year. You guessed it, yours truly.

I broke out in a cold sweat thinking of how close I came to not keeping my commitment. How close I came to breaking my promise.

The Lesson: *If you make a commitment, keep it.* —James J Howard

*Define* what you want . . .

The decisions you make determine the schedule you keep. The schedule you keep determines the life you live. And how you live your life determines how you spend your soul. —Lysa Terkeurst

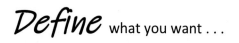*Define* what you want . . .

Confidence comes from consistency, and consistency comes from high-level habits. —Trish Blackwell

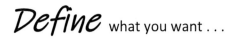 *Define* what you want . . .

Momentum is not the result of one push. It is the result of many continual pushes.
—John Maxwell

Define what you want . . .

Live less out of habit and more out of intent. —Unknown

Define your *Strengths.*

To succeed in life, we must stay within our strength zone but continually move outside our comfort zone. —John Maxwell

Strengths define us and are meant to be shared in a bright, brilliant, and bold fashion.

What are your greatest strengths on which you need to focus?

What do you naturally do well?

Which talents, skills, and gifts do you possess?

What is your niche that sets you apart?

What gives you the greatest return and reward?

How do you use this strength on a daily basis in your life?

Describe what your strength zone is. What success and failures have you had that reinforce that?

How could you align your greatest strength(s) with your strongest belief to make a difference in the life of another person?

Anything else?

Intentionally own it!

What will it take for you to stay in your sweet spot, to understand what you naturally do well and then show up in a bold and brilliant way?

Strengths

[Brilliantly Grounded Wisdom prepared by Cyndi Lesher]

While we try to teach our children all about life, our children teach us what life is all about.

Recently I was walking to the park with my two-year-old grandson. He stopped suddenly and yelled, "Oh, look Nana, aren't the flowers 'boo-ti-ful'?" He was so happy expressing his joy over something he found so amazing. It brought tears to my eyes. But it also *made me pay attention to what I was taking for granted.* Were it not for him, I would have walked right on by those flowers without appreciating their beauty. I decided to try and look at the world through the eyes of a two-year-old.

When you are two, you are new to the world, so everything is amazing. That's a pretty fabulous way to view the world.

Later on his mother was telling me that when he wakes up in the morning, he stands up in his crib and yells, "Hey guys, it's me. I awake!" What a lovely way to begin a day; Look out world, I'm ready to see and be seen! He's a joyful kid. And he's helping me be a joyful adult.

The Lesson: Look at the world through the eyes of a two-year-old. *"It's me! I awake!"*

 *Define* what you want . . .

You don't get harmony when everybody sings the same note. —Doug Floyd

Define what you want . . .

Be the person who sets the tone. When you're passionate about what you do, it's contagious. —Dave Ramsey

 *Define* what you want . . .

I do what's right because I know it's the right thing to do. —Jimmy Carter

Define what you want . . .

Be You! The world will adjust. —Unknown

Define your *True North.*

There's something that is deep within that you're wired to do and be good at.

Many of us live a couple layers above our True North. The busyness of life can crowd out our time to discover it. When you choose to unlock who you are, it will provide you with a source of deep energy, and a clear framework for making decisions about what priorities you should set.

In *The Power of Purpose* by Richard Leider, he shares *The Purpose Formula: Gifts + Passions + Values = Calling*

He encourages you to ask yourself: *Are you using your gifts on things that you feel passionate about, in environments that fit your values?*

When you think of your personal purpose in life, what comes to mind?

What does this mean to you?

What matters the most to you? What is it that you love to do? What makes you come alive from the inside?

What are your innate strengths?

What do you cry about, sing about, dream about? When you layer this with your natural strengths and beliefs, what picture do you see?

Where do you add the greatest value?

How will you measure your life?

How does the purpose of your True North influence your life and decisions?

Anything else?

Intentionally own it!

When you land on your True North, what will it take for you to confidently run like crazy toward it?

True North

[Brilliantly Grounded Wisdom prepared by Cyndi Lesher]

Your True North is your foundation on which your beliefs, values, behaviors, and thoughts are based. Think of it as *your own personal bedrock.*

Your True North guides you in good times and bad times, in sickness and health, in joys and in sorrow. When you are tested—and you will be—*your True North grounds you.*

In my experience, I have found that *knowing your True North is critical to good mental, physical, and spiritual health.* Yet, we often take it for granted or don't figure it out until crisis hits—in the emergency room, in hospice, during trauma, during loss.

When you've defined and live your True North everything is better. You know *what you stand for and what matters to you.* So, joy is greater; tough decisions are easier; your values are clearer; life is more fulfilling.

It has been my experience that your True North develops as you develop. As you gain experience and depth. You don't just wake up on a Thursday morning and know your True North.

True North is *very personal and develops over time.* It is like working out at the gym—the longer you do it, the better you get and the stronger you are.

When I mentor young professionals, I spend a lot of time on this concept as it is the basis for everything else you do personally and professionally. True North develops differently for different people.

I urge people to start young because it makes the journey so much deeper and easier.

If you know what you stand for it gives you perspective and control not only in the good times, but especially in the messy times.

I have a good friend, Gary, who recently ended up in the emergency room, then the intensive care unit, having a quadruple bypass. While he was recovering, we had many long talks about his medical crisis and subsequent recovery. I asked him if he was scared when he was in ER then ICU.

He said, "Cyndi, I was never scared, but I was overwhelmed with regret and remorse. I wish I would have figured out what was important to me and what I needed to do, before I was faced with the possibility of never being able to realize it."

You see, Gary found his True North during a crisis and regretted not having worked on it before age 60 in ICU.

Start early and live your True North.

If you are on the road to nowhere, find another road. —Ashanti Proverb

---

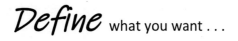 *Define* what you want . . .

Go forward in life with a twinkle in your eye and a smile on your face, but with great and strong purpose in your heart. —Gordon B. Hinkley

 *Define* what you want . . .

We are all rough drafts of the people we're still becoming. —Bob Goff

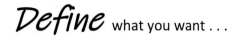 *Define* what you want . . .

When I stand before God at the end of my life, I'd hope I'd not have a single bit of talent left and I could say, "I used everything you gave me." —Erma Bombeck

 *Define* what you want . . .

Don't be mean; it makes mean people look normal. —Bob Goff

Define your *Tribe.*

There's a mental sharpness that comes from being around good people. As Oprah has shared, *"Surround yourself with only people who will lift you higher."*

Who are the people in your life that lift you higher, that challenge you to reach and not settle?

Who are the people that you trust? What makes you trust them and share your heart with them?

Who are your good thinking partners, people that stimulate deeper and bigger thinking, moving your purpose and plans forward?

Who makes you feel bigger after spending time with them?

Who are the people in your life that believe in themselves, which naturally allows them to believe in you too?

Who makes you laugh?

Which people are a fun and positive influence in your life?

Which people in your life align with your values and beliefs?

Which people keep you grounded and centered as a person?

Anything else?

Intentionally own it!

The people we surround ourselves with either raise or lower our standards. They help us become the best-version-of-ourselves or encourage us to become lesser versions of ourselves.

Create a list of those that raise your standards. The people you want and need in your tribe. What will you do to *intentionally* carve out time to spend with them?

Tribe

[Brilliantly Grounded Wisdom prepared by Cyndi Lesher]

My good friend Eileen has had some rough patches over the last fifteen years. She was laid off from her dream job. Her husband decided he didn't want to be married anymore, left her, and decided what he really wanted was to be married to someone else and on it goes.

I have been an understanding and supportive friend, being there when she needed me and even when she didn't think she did.

Things haven't been going well for Eileen over the last several years. After having coffee with her one day it occurred to me that Eileen is eternally bitter, letting past problems block present happiness, and that she works hard at being bitter. What a hard way to live! It sucks the energy out of her and causes difficulty in her friendships.

One day I got up the courage to tell Eileen just that. She reacted with anger and denial, which I had anticipated.

A month went by, and Eileen finally called me to have coffee. We met, and she told me how mad she was that I gave her that feedback. She said it took her time to process it, then she started asking people close to her if they thought she was a bitter person. All confirmed what I had told her.

She said it rocked her world because she had no clue she was stuck in bitterness. She didn't want to be that person and is getting counseling to be better. Then, she thanked me for having the courage to give her the feedback. She said, "*Turns out it's the best gift anyone has ever given me.*"

The lesson: Have the compassion to have courageous conversations with people you care about. *Be brave enough to start a conversation that matters.*

When you speak from the heart, you reach the heart. Don't tell the truth, feel the truth.

Define what you want . . .

Surround yourself with people who make you hungry for life, touch your heart and nourish your soul. —Author Unknown

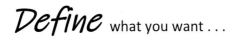

Define what you want . . .

we are the average of the five people we spend the most time with. —Jim Rohn

Define what you want . . .

Be the type of person you want to meet! —Unknown

Define 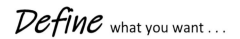 what you want . . .

I just make it my business to get along with people so I can have fun. It's that simple. —Betty White

Define your *Legacy Statement.*

Know the legacy you want to leave—your legacy of leadership in your home, your community, and your place of work.

John Maxwell shares, "People will remember you in one statement. What you do and *how* you do it will determine what they will say."

What do you want that statement to be? Write it out in detail and *live it each day.*

Look at your hands . . .

What's the legacy you want them to leave behind?

What do they represent and what do you want them to represent in your lifetime?

What story have they written thus far?

What stories do you want them to continue to write and not write?

What do you want them to accomplish, work for, create, develop, and lead?

What untapped potential do they still need to pursue?

How do you want them to handle the ups and downs of life?

How will they express love and compassion?

With what kindness will they be involved?

Intentionally own it!

What's one thing you want people to remember about how you impacted their life? Write it out in detail and *live it each day.*

Legacy Statement

[Brilliantly Grounded Wisdom prepared by Cyndi Lesher]

One day I was going to a meeting at Children's Hospital. I was in a hurry and irritated because I got stuck in traffic and was running late. I was hurrying down the hall when I saw an obviously sick 7 or 8 year-old boy walking down the hall, dragging an IV pole. He looked at me with a huge smile and said, "Hi, lady. How are you?" I replied, "You know, I'm just fine now."

That little boy knew what was important.

The Lesson: *Be more like children.*

Children live in the moment because that's all they know. Elders do it because they know time is running out. And living in the present is what makes people happy. —Ashton Applewhite.

*Define* what you want . . .

I don't want to get to the end of my life and find that I lived the length of it. I want to have lived the width of it as well. —Diane Ackerman

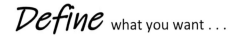

Define what you want . . .

Every man dies; not every man truly lives. —Braveheart

 *Define* what you want . . .

Beginning today, treat everyone you meet as if they were going to be dead by midnight. Extend to them all the care, kindness, and understanding you can muster. And do it with no thought of any reward. Your life will never be the same again. —Og Mandino

Define what you want . . .

Legacy is not leaving something for people, it's leaving something in people. —Peter Strople

Define the picture of your *Dream.*

It takes a lot of courage to show your dreams to someone else. —Erma Bombeck

A dream is an inspiring picture of the future that energizes your mind, will, and emotions. It will enlarge your tenacity and your thinking. You'll do everything you can to achieve it.

What is the thing in your heart that you really want to do?

What stirs you from the inside?

What would you love to accomplish in your life?

What are your reasons for pursuing this dream?

How does this dream excite you?

What are you doing to realize it?

What makes you believe that you were made to bring this dream to life?

How does your dream play to your strengths? Align with what you value?

What would it take to make your dream reality?

How committed are you to bringing this dream forward?

If you chose not to move your dream ahead, where do you think you would stand, long-term, with that decision?

Anything else?

Intentionally own it!

What habits do you have that help you draw closer to your dream? What's one thing you can do, today, to make your dream a reality tomorrow?

Dream

[Brilliantly Grounded Wisdom prepared by Cyndi Lesher]

A Native American proverb says, *"People move toward that which is envisioned."*

To me that means you need a vision and a dream if you want to accomplish something. It is important to be specific, so you know where you're headed and when you get there.

It takes *imagination, motivation, and big thinking.*

I recently read about how college students are flocking to a course on happiness at the University of Pennsylvania. Students are asked to share personal stories about how they have grown as a person. For example, one young woman spoke about how her 95-year old grandma came to live with her family and how the experience forced her to grow as a person. Sharing her story with classmates helped her build deeper connections.

The Penn course focuses on positive psychology, the scientific study of what goes well in life and how to develop more of it.

Imagine a college course focused on personal happiness and developing deeper connections. I think it should be mandatory at all colleges and universities. What a wonderful world it could be!

If we can dream it, it can happen.

Define what you want . . .

Don't get stuck somewhere you should only be passing through. —Christine Cain

Define what you want . . .

Fear is the gatekeeper to strength. —Jill Blashack Strahan

*Define* what you want . . .

Be loyal to your future, not your past. The future depends on what we do in the present.
—Mahatma Gandhi

Define what you want . . .

A dream is a wish your heart makes. —Walt Disney

Define your *Vision.*

"Beginning with the end in mind is based on imagination. If you don't make a conscious effort to visualize who you are and what you want in life, then you empower other people and circumstances to shape you and your life by default." —Stephen Covey

One of the main reasons why most people don't get what they want is they haven't decided what they want. *Get clear on what you want and write it down.*

What does ten years from now look like to you? Five years? Three years? One year?

Why is this important to you? What will it bring to you?

What is it that you most want to celebrate at the end of *this* year?

Why is this important to you? What will it bring to you?

What is it that you most want in each category below? What is your bottom line for each? Describe where your priorities, in each of these areas, stand today.

- Home
- Work
- Family
- Friends
- Finances
- Health/wellness
- Fun & adventure
- Hobbies
- Faith/spiritual
- Self
- Anything else

Intentionally own it!

Decide what you want, review it constantly, and each day do one thing that moves you toward your vision.

Vision

[Brilliantly Grounded Wisdom prepared by Cyndi Lesher]

Visions hold power—the power to see beyond the present and look into the future. You can create visions and a journey to realize them. They are important because they *expand your thinking and help you see in terms of possibilities not obstacles.*

Your work is to discover your world and then with all your heart give yourself to it. —Buddha

I struggled with understanding vision and its power until one day I was visiting the Southwest Initiative Foundation and saw this plaque on the wall: "*The true meaning of life is to plant trees, under whose shade you do not expect to sit.*" —Nelson Henderson

Suddenly, I understood vision. I'm now busy planting trees.

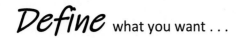*Define* what you want . . .

We don't drift in good direction. We discipline and prioritize ourselves there. —Andy Stanley

*Define* what you want . . .

Ten years from now make sure you can say you chose your life, you didn't settle for it.
—Mandy Hale

Define what you want . . .

Every choice you make determines the standards of your life. —Joe Duncan

 *Define* what you want . . .

We often lose who we are while trying to become someone we aren't. —Nicki Koziarz

*Define* what you want . . .

Every person has a longing to be significant, to make a contribution, to be part of something noble and purposeful. —John Maxwell

Define what you want . . .

Let your smile change the world. Don't let the world change your smile.
We shall never know all the good that a simple smile can do. —Mother Teresa

Define your *Goals.*

Goals give your vision, dreams, and values momentum. Goals create a plan of action.

The structure and habits that are formed to move your goals forward is where the magic lies. Goals are designed to shape you as you go from where you are to where you intend to be.

In which area(s) of your life do you want to grow and expand?

Why is this important to you?

Do you know how to grow and expand in these areas?

Imagine one year from now. What do you plan to see as growth in your life?

When you intentionally grow, what will this bring to all aspects of your life?

Are you willing to do the work to make this picture reality?

What are your large lifetime goals?

What are your smaller daily goals?

In which ways do you intentionally ensure they align?

How are your goals aligned with your values? Dreams? Vision? Priorities?

What will you do to ensure you are moving toward purposeful targets?

Anything else?

Intentionally own it!

What is your Personal Growth Plan?

Intentionally commit to growing personally every day. *Each day* do *ONE thing* that moves you toward your goals. What will it take for you to adopt this practice? What will hold you back? How do you overcome this potential obstacle?

Goals

[Brilliantly Grounded Wisdom prepared by Cyndi Lesher]

I think a lot more about aging than I ever used to, probably because I have more history than future.

Remember when you were a little kid and someone asked your age you would reply, "I'm 7-and-a-half!" Well, I thought my days of counting the halves were over, but recently I find myself counting halves again. I think it is because time feels like it's going at warp speed and the halves *help me set and mark goals.*

I find the process of setting goals and checking progress makes me feel like I'm accomplishing a lot. And, I am. It just makes me feel *happier, more productive, and future-focused.* All good, I think.

Back in those "half" years I would say things to my mom like, "I wish it was Christmas; I wish it was my birthday; I wish it was summer . . ." and my mom would say, "Cyndi, don't wish your life away."

I never quite got what she was saying to me until I hit the adult years. Then, one day I heard myself saying to my own child, "Lindsey, don't wish your life away." I get it now! Big time!

I think that, in life and in careers, goal setting is valuable. It helps you accomplish more, because you hold yourself accountable and can see progress, or lack thereof. Obviously, it is very motivating when you see progress or accomplish a goal or milestone. Conversely, when you don't see progress or accomplish the goal it is easy to give up. *DON'T LET YOURSELF give up.*

Readjust your goal; *figure out what is getting in the way.* What are you doing to hold yourself accountable?

It is important for teams to have goals. Groups too. And families. *It helps you move toward something and helps you to stay focused*, keeping your eye on the prize.

And it is a joyful way to work individually or as a team when you are working toward accomplishing something small or large.

Little kids in kindergarten will do almost anything reasonable to get a sticker for an accomplishment. They love them and are so proud of themselves. I'm thinking we maybe should get stickers as adults.

We need to feel happy and proud *for accomplishing something. Not just for showing up.* Think about it. Seriously.

The Lesson: Stickers aren't just for kids. *All people want to accomplish things and feel valued.*

Questions to ponder:

> Think of areas of your life where setting goals could be helpful. Set a goal and decide how you will hold yourself accountable

> Do you get "stickers" in your life? How do you celebrate accomplishments?

> Do you give other people "stickers" for goal attainment? If not, how open are you to blending this into your way of encouraging others?

*Define* what you want . . .

Encouragement is oxygen to the soul. Don't ever get too busy to encourage others.
—John Maxwell

Define what you want . . .

Don't take the agenda that someone else has mapped out for your life. —John Maxwell

Define what you want . . .

Never underestimate the compounding effect of CONSISTENCY. —John Maxwell

Define what you want . . .

Look at everything in a positive way. Negativity is noise! —Tory Burch

Define your *Thoughts.*

The mind leads the body, not the other way around. We literally become what we think about.

Your self-image (subconscious picture of yourself) determines . . .

Your performance (how you behave or perform) stimulates . . .

Your self-talk (what you say to yourself about your performance) forms and reinforces . . .

Your self-image. Your I AM.

The greatest indicator of anybody's future is their self-image. How you see yourself will determine what you get out of life. *You'll never outperform your self-image!*

Research indicates that on average, people talk to themselves about 50,000 times each day. Unfortunately, this self-talk is 80 percent negative. *No matter what our success might be, we rarely allow ourselves to appreciate our victories. We are built so the negative screams and the positive only whispers.*

Through research, we also know that these thoughts have a powerful effect on us. They affect our attitudes, motivation, physiology, and even our biochemistry.

Every cell in your body is affected by every thought you have.

Questions to ask yourself to boost your self-image:

What is it about your life that you enjoy and like?

Which people in your life make you feel special?

What is one thing you can do today to make a positive impact in somebody else's life? (*The greatest way to build self-image is to help someone else.*)

When you think of positive qualities, which ones do you want in your life?

What is it that comes naturally to you?

What are the good things happening in your life? What are the wins?

What's something you have done that makes you feel good from the inside out?

What are you doing today to intentionally grow and sharpen who you are?

Define your *Thoughts.*

Out of the many investments we can make in life, the most important one you and I will ever make is in ourselves. That investment will determine what we get out of life.

Furthermore, one key area in which we must make an investment is the quality of our thoughts. The number one reason people do not reach their potential in life is due to their thinking. If we allow limiting beliefs to consume our thoughts, they will have an absolute negative impact on every area of our lives.

What limiting beliefs do you often deal with?

Describe your current way of thinking? Where do you focus your thoughts?

Where in life are you failing to get the results you want?

What aspects of your thinking might be leading to these results?

What changes in your thinking might be required to produce the good results you desire?

Do you know why this shift in thinking is important to you?

What processes and practices will you adopt that will stimulate productive thinking?

Do you know how to make the shift happen?

Where do you stand when it comes to the priority of relationships today?

In which ways does intentionally spending time with good people improve your overall health and happiness? How could you bring more of this into your life?

Where and when will you choose to intentionally create your thoughts?

Anything else about your thinking life that you need to face and move through?

Intentionally own it!

What commitment will you make to yourself to ensure you positively influence your self-image every day? When you do, what will be the benefit to you and those in your life?

Ways to lift Your *Thinking* . . .

Gratitude!

What is your honest assessment of your current daily gratitude level? What would it look like to adopt a daily habit of logging the good that is happening in your life every day?

Daily affirmations!

What would it look like to embrace a positive mindset and self-talk routine each morning and evening—to create an attitude of expectancy that good things will happen to you, and through you, each day?

Look up. Notice. Act!

What would it look like to spread kindness and goodness to others, every day—with no expectations of recognition or reward? Set an unselfish goal to consciously add value to three people every day. Be an intentional daymaker! (*Everyone you know needs three things: encouragement, appreciation, and recognition. It's oxygen to the soul.*)

Prayer. Meditation!

What would it look like to start each day in prayer and/or mediation—to be intentional about staying connected to your core and the values that ground you?

Reflect!

What would it look like to intentionally carve out time to practice the discipline of daily reflective thinking— a time to think, land your thoughts, ask yourself questions into the area/s in which you want to grow and discern your way forward? What would this practice bring to your life?

Live generously!

What would it look like to be wildly generous with your time and/or money? What type of difference would that make, in your life, and in the lives of others?

Thinking

[Brilliantly Grounded Wisdom prepared by Cyndi Lesher]

My beloved brother-in-law died suddenly. He was my favorite of my husband's brothers. Don't get me wrong, I like them all, but it always felt like Leo and I had a special connection.

Several days after his death, we got a sympathy card in the mail—a PAPYRUS card. It is a beautiful card from long-time, loving friends. I read the little flyer that came with the card telling you to protect the delicate handwork by placing the paper over the front of the card before inserting it into the envelope.

It read: "*Legends say that hummingbirds float free of time, carrying our hopes for love, joy, and celebration. The hummingbird's delicate grace reminds us that life is rich, beauty is everywhere, every personal connection has meaning, and that laughter is life's sweetest creation.*"

That held so much meaning for me, it made me cry. Then it made me laugh. What a perfect description of loved ones and God's grace in our lives.

When I think of Leo, I will always see a hummingbird. *Recognize and appreciate the hummingbirds in your life.*

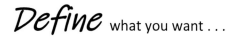 *Define* what you want . . .

Courage is not the absence of fear, but rather the assessment that something else is more important than fear. —Franklin D. Roosevelt

Define what you want . . .

All the resources we need are in our mind. —Theodore Roosevelt

 what you want . . .

There is an abundant need in this world for your exact brand of beautiful. —Lysa TerKeurst

Define what you want . . .

Remember, no one has it all together. —Unknown

Define your *Leadership.*

To lead any way, other than by example, we send a fuzzy picture of leadership to others.
—John Maxwell

Knowing that leadership is influence—nothing more, nothing less—how are you currently influencing those around you?

Is that the type of leadership influence/example you would want to be around?

What is *your* personal definition of leadership?

What do you believe makes a person a good leader? Are you showing up that way? If not, why?

Ray Kroc has stated that, "*The quality of a leader is reflected in the standards they set for themselves.*"
> What expectations do you have of yourself as a person? As a leader? What are the standards to which you hold yourself? How does this add value to those around you?

What do you want your leadership style and brand to convey? What does this style of leadership mean to you?

In which areas of leadership must you expand and grow? How will you intentionally make this happen?

How will you continually measure your influence as a leader to ensure that it's lining up with your values and personal picture of leadership?

What would get in your way of being the type of influential leader you picture yourself being?

Anything else?

Intentionally own it!

John Maxwell has shared, "*Everything rises and falls on leadership.*" With this mindset, in which ways are you modeling leadership well? In which areas must you intentionally tighten it up?

Leadership

[Brilliantly Grounded Wisdom prepared by Cyndi Lesher]

It seems like everything you read or hear about comes back to leadership.

You hear about the lack of leadership, the abuse of leadership, the power of leadership, the importance of leadership. *Leadership principles always involve values, purpose, vision,* and *refined character.*

In my experience, the LEADER makes everything come together and *inspires people to do their best.* When that happens, great things happen; people deliver great results.

The leader sets the vision toward which to strive. A Native American proverb I read years ago and continue to practice states: "*People move toward that which is envisioned.*" That's what leadership is and what a leader does. A leader sets the vision, rules, or guidelines, then *holds themselves* and everyone else accountable.

It's actually pretty simple when you think about it. Then why is it so hard to do in reality? Probably because people are sometimes reluctant to take calculated risks. That's why an effective leader makes things happen.

The lesson: "*You can't be that kid standing at the top of the waterslide, overthinking it. You have to go down the chute.*" —Tina Fey

Questions to ponder:

Think about effective leaders you have known and worked with. What traits made them an effective leader?

Are you seeing those same traits show up in your personal style of leadership? If not, how can you use them to influence others?

Individuals can be leaders without a leadership title. Why are individual leaders important? What traits do they have? How are you contributing as an individual everyday leader?

 *Define* what you want . . .

When your actions inspire others to dream more, learn more, do more, and become more, you are a leader. —John Quincy Adams

Define what you want . . .

Leadership is a behavior, not a title. — Gordon Hanson

Leadership is not about titles, positions, or flowcharts. It's about one life influencing another. —John Maxwell

 *Define* what you want . . .

Your capacity to grow will determine your capacity to lead. —John Maxwell

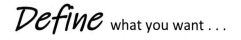*Define* what you want . . .

The most powerful leadership tool you have is your own personal example. —John Wooden

Define how you'll make it *Real!*

Life is too short to spend your days out of sync with your own heart. —Waylon Lewis

As you move into the stage of taking what you wrote and making it real, let's circle back to the word *imagine.*

Let yourself get into that mindset again.

Imagine . . .

>   knowing who you are from the inside out and bringing that forward;
>
>   being grounded by your internal anchors;
>
>   reaching your potential in life;
>
>   believing in yourself and loving who you are;
>
>   thinking inward to confidently write a life story that is YOU. Truly. You.

Allow this guide to be a tidy spot for you to continue to consciously land your thinking and keep logging what you want to bring forward in life—no matter what stage you're at. Circle back on it often, believing it will happen.

By continuing to use this guide to integrate self-leadership into your core identity, you'll be able to navigate through different phases of life (both the highs and lows) in a grounded state of mind, in a manner that anchors your resilience and decision making from within.

Dare to be the coach of your life and let your hands continue to write a story that is *original* and *true* to you.

As John Maxwell has shared, "You can live your life any way you want, but you can only live it once."

Intentionally own it!

Use the space below to begin drafting your personalized path forward, asking yourself, "How will I intentionally bring forward in life what I most want?"

Growth is not natural. That's why we must be intentional about defining what we want and each day do one thing to move it forward.

Making it Real

[Brilliantly Grounded Wisdom prepared by Cyndi Lesher]

I love Ellen DeGeneres's humor and authenticity. People think of her only as a comedian because they may not know her backstory. She is an advocate for *helping people "live their truths."* (*Grit and Grace* – Pauline Weger and Alicia Williamson)

Making it real is *living authentically true to yourself and your values.* It is too hard to try to fake it, and people can spot a fake. It's just too hard not to be real.

Being real is a rollup of your values, your character . . . who you are.

I didn't figure this out until my 40s. I tried too hard to be who other people thought I should be—to fit the corporate image, to do everything well in my roles as wife, mother, employee, leader, and on it goes. Then one day I came to a blinding obvious conclusion: *Everyone else thought I was great, but I DIDN'T FEEL GOOD ABOUT ME.*

I felt like an imposter living my life.

And you know what? I decided to start living an authentic life.

Once I began living intentionally in this area, I felt great. *I liked who I was.* I felt joy again, and I committed to *"live my truth."* I don't think many people noticed the difference, but I sure did.

"Care. Love. Be Outraged. Be Devastated. Just Don't Give Up. *The world needs good humans today."* —Ellen DeGeneres

Define what you want . . .

We cannot become what we need to be by remaining what we are. —John Maxwell

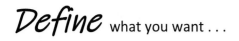 *Define* what you want . . .

I will not follow where the path may lead, but will go where there is no path, and I will leave a trail. —Muriel Strode

Define what you want . . .

The goal is to continue to change, and never change in the same way twice. —Taylor Swift

Define what you want . . .

People who end up as "first" don't actually set out to be first. They set out to do something they love. —Condoleezza Rice

Brilliantly
Grounded Wisdom

Brilliantly Grounded Wisdom

He said, "You become. It takes a long time. That's why it doesn't happen often to people who break easily, or have sharp edges, or who have to be carefully kept. Generally, by the time you are Real, most of your hair has been loved off, and your eyes drop out and you get loose in the joints and very shabby. But these things don't matter at all, because once you are Real you can't be ugly, except to the people who don't understand." —The Velveteen Rabbit

With tremendous grace and courage, the following leaders have chosen to direct and design the *impact* of their life story. They have chosen to put themselves in it. To be the author. To intentionally influence the many different phases of their life.

Our hands reflect our choices in life. They draft a story that will someday be the legacy of our life and leadership—in our homes, our community, and in our places of work. They "do" what our head and heart has led them to pursue.

Their wisdom is rooted in what they have experienced, observed, and *chosen to learn* thus far. Each have intentionally made a meaningful mark of significance in the lives of many, many people – including mine.

It is our sincere desire that their candid insight will inspire you to boldly design a life that is *original to you*!

(Connect with their stories under Encouragement at www.bar33leadership.com.)

Life is amazing if you don't let it weaken you. —Geanne Panktratz

**Introductions for each grounded wisdom contributor were written by Alyssa Kreutzfeldt.

Brilliantly Grounded Wisdom [Prepared by . . . Howard Feiertag]

I met Howard back in 1999 when I was working in the hospitality industry. He wrote articles for a magazine I frequently read, and I always thought, "I will meet him someday."

That someday came when Don Peterson, the general manager I worked for, agreed to fly me to Howard's workshop in Dallas, Texas. He has been a special part of my life ever since.

At this moment, we find Howard at the age of 91 still teaching a few days a week at Virginia Tech and releasing yet another book he has written.

When we talk about intentionality—adopting a growth mindset and embracing a positive stance for life—he is one we can all aspire to be a bit more like. I know I do!

When I talked with Howard to capture his insight, these are the rich lessons this vibrant leader, of almost a century, shares with us:

Being the youngest of ten children and the only one that went on to college, Howard's story is about *choosing a positive attitude and always believing in your ability,* whether you are supported by others or not.

He is confident that his success has come from helping other people become better—*by making a difference in their lives, it has in turn, made a difference in his.* This was not a mindset he was raised with, it's one he took on himself in life.

Throughout his lengthy career, he's found that people followed him not because of his education or background, but because of who he is. No one has ever looked at his resume; they've always been attracted to his attitude and results.

He's a master at creating cultures that people want to be part of, because he knows how to *influence momentum and listen to people.*

His spirit of always helping others to be successful is contagious.

Because he believes so strongly in the power of others, he designed the Starfish Award—it's given out to those who make a difference in someone else's life.

[Continued by . . . Howard Feiertag]

Howard chooses to live a life where he *remains positive about everything*. He decided years back to not worry, complain, gossip, judge, or create negativity. His stance is to look for the good in life, and this perspective has provided him with healthy relationships, opportunities, and mindset.

He believes in *taking time for people—to listen well, not by offering suggestions for improvement, yet simply listening*.

As he works with college students, he often shares this advice:

- Choose to *know what's good about you*. Be confident.
- *Prove it!* Get started. Learn something. Do a great job. Don't worry about your salary or the next steps—prove yourself first! The next steps will come when you do a great job where you're at—and you'll get paid.

Howard is always offering a bright smile and the opportunity to mentor those in his life. He's intentionally chosen to be a positive impact.

Brilliantly Grounded Wisdom [Prepared by . . . Robin Kocina]

Robin is a wife, mother, grandmother, and, professionally, owner of Media Relations (now semi-retired).

Robin became a dear friend and mentor of mine over fifteen years ago. She has received many professional accolades yet always carves out time to mentor and guide those around her in a sincere and heartfelt fashion.

Our hands write our life story. When you look at your hands, what type of story do they represent?

> My hands remind me of my mother's hands and the lessons in tenacity and persistence that she's taught me.

At what point in your life did you learn to really know and embrace who you are and choose to live intentionally—in all areas?

> Several major life events happened when I was in my twenties. Living intentionally became a priority at that time. *You can decide where you want your life to go and, with God's guidance, you can make it happen.*
>
> I believe we can set our intentions and make them happen, despite the inevitable detours. I have lived my whole life this way and it has worked, starting back to my early twenties when I decided I should be an accountant. I was a single mom with no money for school, but I found a way.
>
> This led to great jobs at Cargill and then when my dad got sick in my late twenties, I quit to run his business, a sawmill. At that moment, I learned that I have the skills to be an entrepreneur and that's what I should be.
>
> *You can look into the future and set your intentions, or you can just go whichever way the wind blows.* A burning desire does not just happen. It starts with a spark and becomes a flame by setting your intention. You cultivate it; you turn it into a burning desire; you make it happen.
>
> I think a lot of people think it's too hard, and it's easier just to go with whatever happens. *Without being intentional, other people are controlling your life and destiny.*

[Continued...Robin Kocina]

What helped develop your character and your values?

My relationship with God. I read the Bible daily. I love being in the Word.

Every day, I learn something from reading scriptures and devotions *that enable me to stay focused on the positive.*

When you look at your life . . .

What has mattered the most? My relationship with God. That gives me a better understanding of my other personal relationships. I surround myself with positive messages and choose to spend time around positive people *because goodness breeds goodness.*

What has surprised you? My natural inclination is to hurry and to multitask, to power through everything on my to-do list. But I've learned I can *slow down, work with intention, and still get things done.*

What would you look at differently? Detours. When we're younger, we expect life to follow a straight line. But God puts uncomfortable detours in our path for a reason. Maybe it's to teach us an important lesson about ourselves or to guide us toward a better opportunity.

When I look back at my life, it's easy to see that the things *that were upsetting turned out to be valuable direction changers.*

What type of advice would you share with your 30-year-old self?

Slow down. Celebrate your strengths and celebrate other people's strengths. Look for the positive. *Don't clutter your thoughts or your life with negative emotions or negative people.* Spend time each day with the Bible and in prayer.

Brilliantly Grounded Wisdom [Prepared by . . . Steve Willock]

Steve is a husband, father, and, professionally, the general manager and director of golf at Oak Marsh Golf Course.

As a hospitality degree major at North Dakota State University, I met Steve at a college career fair. He recruited me to join the opening team at Oak Marsh Golf Course. By saying "yes!" to his invitation, I was led to my husband, Fred!!

I have always admired Steve's calm demeanor and his sincere commitment to the people in his life, including his family.

Our hands write our life story. When you look at your hands, what type of story do they represent?

My hands represent hard work. They are always open to shake someone's hand or to help them in need. They are folded in prayer, daily, thanking the Lord for standing by my side.

At what point in your life did you learn to really know and embrace who you are and choose to live intentionally—in all areas?

Still a work in progress. I've probably always talked a little more than necessary because I get excited to be with people.

I've been lucky to find my passion (golf) and make it my living—traveling around the world, following the golf business, staying involved, and meeting many wonderful people.

What helped develop your character and your values?

Definitely my mother and father, for teaching my brother, sisters, and me right from wrong. *They led by example* and showed us what hard work looked like. I've also had numerous mentors that showed me examples of what each day could bring.

[Continued by . . . Steve Willock]

When you look at your life . . .

What has mattered the most? Absolutely my relationship with the Lord and my relationship with my wife, Roslyn, who is my best friend.

What has surprised you? The kindness of all people, once you peel back the layers. *I still believe everyone has good in their heart*, some just have it hidden behind problems or barriers we don't see.

What would you look at differently? The amount of time I give to all others and neglect the ones that deserve it the most (the Lord and my family).

What type of advice would you share with your 30-year-old self?

Carve out more time for prayer, family, and self-relaxation. Life is truly short. *Money can't buy happiness.*

Anything else?

If you like winning, *Positivity Wins . . . and it's contagious!!*

Brilliantly Grounded Wisdom [Prepared by . . . Rob Amundson]

Rob is a husband, father, and, professionally, has held various executive positions in sales leadership.

Our paths met while in the hospitality business. I worked under his leadership and was drawn to his contagious positive attitude and passion for people. His leadership created an environment you wanted to be part of.

Our hands write our life story. When you look at your hands, what type of story do they represent?

> Hard work! My hands are scarred, busted up, and always sore. It's a story of starting work young and doing the types of jobs that required physical work.

At what point in your life did you learn to really know and embrace who you are and choose to live intentionally—in all areas? ·

> I was always very goal orientated. But *being goal orientated and being intentional are two different things.*

> I have a naturally competitive spirit and when I went into things, I was already comparing myself to others and analyzing where the next opportunity or step would be. That led me down some paths where I *appeared to be successful, but it really wasn't where I wanted to be or where I was happy.*

> I achieved goals but somehow, I felt those were goals that others put on me and I didn't necessarily choose for myself.

> I really became intentional when I realized I wasn't happy in my personal life or career and took the very difficult steps to *begin the journey to define myself.* I can tell you the exact place I was when I made that decision! It's as clear to me today as it was then. I have been very intentional ever since!

What helped develop your character and your values?

> My upbringing—parents, teachers, and coaches. I grew up in an era where your neighbors didn't hesitate to discipline you or call you out for your behavior.

[Continued by . . . Rob Amundson]

I was the last of five kids, so I also had four people over me who kept me on my toes. I always felt a strong sense of responsibility and always to do the right thing. That intensified when my sister was diagnosed with a rare blood disorder and literally spent years in the hospital.

By then most of my siblings had moved out, so I was left on my own from junior high to high school. During that time my dad lost his business and began to develop early-onset Alzheimer's. All those things had a very profound effect on who I am and what to this day I deem important.

When you look at your life . . .

What has mattered the most? Family and friends. Losing a sister and parent early in life really formed a realization that we're not here forever.

What has surprised you? Where I am in life. I literally started over in my late 30s and gave up everything (financially as well), and I am still in awe at *how I grew personally and progressed in my career* to be where I am today.

What would you look at differently? My early decisions. Like I said, *I often did things or followed a path I "thought" was right, but I knew wasn't necessarily what I really wanted.*

What type of advice would you share with your 30-year-old self?

Take more risks! Make decisions and stick to them! Don't be afraid of success.

Anything else?

I look back now on where I came from and where I am, and I can say that I have been very blessed in this life!

Brilliantly Grounded Wisdom [Prepared by . . . Camille Thomas]

Camille is a wife, mother, grandmother, and, professionally, owner of JMC Retail Group.

My connection with Camille was formed through a corporate partnership with WPO (Women Presidents' Organization). Initially, I was drawn to her influential presence and wit. Once I experienced Camille as a friend, I was drawn to her genuine and grounded spirit, tenacity for growth, laughter, and deeply rooted values.

Our hands write our life story. When you look at your hands, what type of story do they represent?

> When I look at my hands, I see a story of *self-respect, respect for others, happiness, grace, and servant leader.*

At what point in your life did you learn to really know and embrace who you are and choose to live intentionally—in all areas?

> When I look back at my life, choosing to live intentionally began at 25 years of age. My boss was diagnosed with AIDS. I watched him wither away, and I knew then how fragile and how special life was for all of us.

What helped develop your character and your values?

> When I look back at character and values, I can say with clarity that family, my husband, and *the team of people I surround myself with each day, build my character and reinforce the values I live by.*

When you look at your life . . .

> **What mattered most?** *Truth to myself* matters most.

> **What has surprised you?** What surprises me is how easy it is to live each day *accepting myself as I am* vs. trying to conform to the next audience or expectation.

[Continued by . . . Camille Thomas]

What type of advice would you share with your 30-year-old self?

When I look at my 30-year-old self, my advice to me is: Slow down! Love each day! Smile more! Pray with gratitude! Find joy!

Anything else?

Live knowing each day you did your best—not only in words but in actions. And be present every day, accepting there is no guarantee for the "perfect" tomorrow.

Brilliantly Grounded Wisdom [Prepared by . . . John Jensvold]

John is a husband, father, and, professionally, an executive in the construction industry.

John was introduced to my life when I interviewed to work for the Chamber of Commerce. Along with Rod, he was the board chair that hired me. Their "offer" was a game-changer for my life, personally and professionally. It helped me understand commerce on a whole different level and, more importantly, allowed me to intentionally make Minneapolis feel like a small town.

Being exposed to John's style of leadership, at such an early stage in my career, provided me with treasured insights that I keep to this day.

Our hands write our life story. When you look at your hands, what type of story do they represent?

> When I stop to notice my hands, they are beginning to look like my father's hands when he was my age, when I was just starting to notice such things, as a six-year-old kid. Their coloration, shape of the fingers, smooth knuckles are all from my dad. The only real difference is that I have spent much of my working life in an office, while he spent much of his working life working with tools. His hands were a little bigger and a lot stronger than mine.

> He's gone now, but our lives resemble one another in many important ways. I am reminded of that fact, examining my hands, and feel grateful.

At what point in your life did you learn to really know and embrace who you are and choose to live intentionally—in all areas?

> *I suppose it would be wonderful to proclaim that I've lived intentionally since my earliest memories,* but nothing could be further from the truth. In all honesty, I am sliding into that zone only now, only now beginning to think in those terms.

> *Perspective is a gift from God* and, looking back, what may have seemed like intentional living in the present was likely just the fatigue of the demands of work,

family, house, bills, deadlines, furnace failures in January, that sort of thing. It wasn't living intentionally; it was dodging bullets and trying to avoid any damaging missteps.

Today it might be different, but I won't know for sure until the future allows me —again to look backward.

I know this: *Life is slowing down a bit for me, and I find myself genuinely interested in people I don't know well.* That seems to be a new fact in my life. I start conversations and offer observations that ordinarily I would have avoided as a waste of effort.

Every day I strive to find some tiny way to improve a mood or lighten a load with a joke or a friendly compliment. There is great energy swirling in our world that drives everything. It needs to be fed with kindness; otherwise it turns poisonous. At a certain age you can see this plainly.

What helped develop your character and your values?

Well, first one must consider what they stand for. I have an embedded desire for fairness but get a little squeamish about charity. I respect *tenacity that lives in a moral framework.* I am drawn to the underdog that overcomes by sheer will.

We are products of our parents, by and large, or products of some deterioration involving parents. I, myself, blossomed out of a traditional two-parent household, blue-collar and proud, where failing to live up to a commitment was unheard of, even when it hurt.

When you look at your life . . .

What has mattered the most? Many things have mattered most in my life, but if I were to find a common denominator in all of them it is this: My wife of twenty-nine years believes in her heart that I would never walk away, however dire the circumstances.

[Continued by . . . John Jensvold]

Whether dealing with ailing parents, raising children, managing through the emotional explosions that accompany three daughters, she believes that I would stand with her in all things. She has more faith in me, frankly, than I deserve, but *her belief matters most to me and I will not jeopardize it.*

What has surprised you? By nature, I am not terribly analytical unless someone requires it of me.

I have made most of the important decisions in my life based on intuition. It surprises me that this approach has for the most part worked out for me, because it appears illogical, even to me. At this point I probably over-value intuition versus data because I have, no doubt, been rather lucky—let's face it.

What would you look at differently? I have been thinking about this question for the past few years and I think I have done a disservice to the role of the church in my life.

For many years I shunned religion because I had lost respect for the institution of the church, feeling it was far too human of an invention to invest in spiritually. Eventually, I conflated the lofty concept of God with the hard reality of the church. In my mind they were merged and empty of value. This was unfortunate and led me on more than one spiritual dead end.

I still have not reconciled with the church or its many servants, but seem to be reconnected with what I feel is God. My heart is more open today than it ever has been, but I wonder *what price my daughters will pay for the path I took*? I'm not certain.

What type of advice would you share with your 30-year-old self?

I turned 30 in 1993. I had been married for three years, living in our second house (a slight upgrade from the first), working at a new job in downtown Minneapolis, with a six-month-old baby suffering from colic and sleeping no more than two hours at a stretch.

[Continued by . . . John Jensvold]

At the time, *I recall being overly concerned about appearances. I wanted to project to the world a sense of stability, of calm, of budding affluence, an emerging "big shot."*

I would say to my 30-year-old self that a streak of immaturity can easily persist in a 30-year-old and should be admitted from time to time, to diminish its influence.

Society screams norms at us every day and, if we listen too closely, we can deceive ourselves, even sadden and disappoint ourselves quite unnecessarily.

Anything else?

The world is sprinkled with wisdom, not too different from a backyard on Easter morning where dozens of plastic eggs with chocolate treats rest under bushes and in the crooks of tree branches.

To walk through that yard and not realize it's Easter, one would likely miss the presence of the eggs altogether. But if expected, you begin to pay closer attention, to glance around.

No matter who or where you are in the world, they are there, specially prepared for only you. Most people miss them. Some find them.

Brilliantly Grounded Wisdom [Prepared by . . . Patsy Levang]

Patsy is a wife, mother, educator, and grandmother. Professionally, she works on her family's farm, is a board member for various organizations, and was instrumental in the development and growth of a Christian charter school in their community.

Throughout the years, I have always admired her connectedness, her ability to drive forward initiatives and results, all while expressing care for those in her life, near or far.

Our hands write our life story. When you look at your hands, what type of story do they represent?

My hands were taught at an early age that hard work garners great success. They were expected to do their share of all mundane, tedious household tasks along with all the outdoor chores to care for the animals on the family farm. *They learned the art of being calm in crisis and being active and motivated to develop energy for more than one task at a time.*

At what point in your life did you learn to really know and embrace who you really are and choose to live intentionally—in all areas?

When I reached my junior year in high school, 1966, and produced a science project, which allowed me to travel to the Miramar Naval Air Station and the Salk Institute in the San Diego area, when Jonas Salk was actively working there.

I believed I could do anything after listening to the world-renowned scientists speak at the Salk Institute. From that experience, I determined to do whatever I did to the best of my ability.

When I entered my senior year in high school, *I knew I wanted to try and do something significant.*

[Continued by . . . Patsy Levang]

Who helped develop your character and the values you stand for?

First, my parents were amazing people, and they taught and trained me to observe many things. Among the things they taught me was to treasure the land we lived on and take care of it.

My parents taught me the *golden rule of treating others with respect just the same way that I wanted to be treated.* Early on, they taught me the entire Ten Commandments and lived them out, to the best of their ability, every day before me.

My high school science teachers made me believe that *if I believed in myself, then I could lead others and do so in a significant way.*

The biggest cementing of my values came a few years later, after I had graduated from my undergraduate studies in psychology and had returned home from graduate school and my postgraduate studies. I met and married my best friend. In our first year of marriage we both agreed we wanted to have a personal relationship with Jesus Christ and by the simple act of asking him into our lives, our focus changed from a self-centered focus to a Christ-centered, others-orientated focus.

When you look at your life . . .

What has mattered most? The relationship I have with Christ has mattered the most. Following Christ, my relationship with my husband has been primary. Following my husband has been my relationship with my children and the people they have chosen to regard well in their lives. Currently, my focus has settled on being a significant role model to my grandchildren.

The set ideas that matter most are those foundational values that cause me to continually weigh out the good, the bad, and the indifferent. *I have come to believe that everything we do, or to what we are exposed, has an intrinsic futuristic claim on our value system.*

Therefore, with that in mind, it is a *daily challenge to make what I do count. There is no time to just waste.*

What has surprised you? Anytime I've been successful, at anything, I am the person most surprised. Even though I have set goals to be successful at various tasks and in various situations, the constancy of surprise is always a part of the final situation.

[Continued by . . . Patsy Levang]

It is alternatively refreshing and pleasant and is often the reason *I am willing to go ahead to the next venture.* For example, I did not plan to write a book, but the situation developed over time and then it just seemed like the natural thing to do. Then the question became, "Why not do it well?" I did, and again the surprise was pleasant.

What would you look at differently? I would not have changed anything. I feel I could have worked a bit harder in college if grades had been more my focus, but back in my time in college, a well-rounded, balanced approach to life was considered equally important.

If anything had been greatly changed, I might not have had the sense of fulfillment and joy at the state of my life today.

What type of advice would you share with your 30-year-old self?

Take time to pay close attention to each event and all the people who have passed through my circle of life. Glean and learn as much as you can from each person and situation.

I would *encourage myself not to be so hard on myself when I felt like I failed at something, because if it weren't for the failures, the successes would be hard to measure and not nearly as sweet.*

I would advise myself to stay fit physically because you will live a long time.

I would suggest several ideas that would develop my leadership skills sooner because, looking back, I was asked to lead before I was really skilled to lead.

I would suggest spending zero time with mean-spirited people, who lie with ease. They are dangerous and will only hurt you.

Last, but not least, I would suggest to myself that I should *show the kind-spirited people around me even more approval and love them more than I did because they were going to be so instrumental in helping me become all that I could be.*

Brilliantly Grounded Wisdom [Prepared by . . . Rick S.]

Rick is a husband, father, grandfather, and, professionally, the co-owner/founder of The Reserve.

While running my business from The Reserve, my conversations with Rick always made me walk away thinking, "What a quality person!" I quickly learned to respect his keen sense for business, his sincere adoration for his family, and the values he brings forth in life.

Our hands write our life story. When you look at your hands, what type of story do they represent?

My story is one of perseverance and hard work coupled with great blessings.

At what point in your life did you learn to really know and embrace who you are and choose to live intentionally—in all areas?

It probably began in my late 30s. While the children were growing up, the business we started crossed over from a survival to high growth mode, providing a sense that the business was going to be successful. At that point, my whole career perspective changed from building a career and wealth to *creating a family legacy for future generations.* (The family legacy part is still a work in progress.)

What helped develop your character and the values you stand for?

I was grounded with sound values from childhood inspired by a disabled mother who had (has) such an *inspiring and positive attitude toward life amidst challenges,* and a grandmother whose work ethic and love was second to none.

Also, I *learned early on that it was just easier to do things right rather than have to explain why you didn't.*

[Continued by . . . Rick S.]

When you look at your life . . .

What has mattered the most? An *inner compass which challenges me to ask myself if I am making the right decisions every day.*

A grounded family life (first children, now grandchildren, and perhaps great-grandchildren in the future) whose values mirror my wife's and my own.

Building businesses which add value to society and in doing so create career opportunities for the employees, the suppliers, the customers, and the shareholders.

What has surprised you? That so many people cut corners in life and try to slip by doing a minimum just to get by. It seems so easy to *apply common sense, work hard, and do the right thing every day.*

What would you look at differently? I really don't live with any regrets.

What type of advice would you share with your 30-year-old self?

Be more patient, be more empathetic, be a better listener, and realize that people are wired differently—and that's what makes life so interesting.

Anything else?

My epitaph: "The world was made a little better because Rick spent some time on this earth."

Brilliantly Grounded Wisdom [Prepared by . . . Shelly Meighan]

Shelly is a wife, mother, grandmother, and, professionally, a retired executive with Principal Financial Group.

When I met Shelly over a decade ago, I was drawn to her personal drive and desire to elevate others. She handled conversations with such grace yet remained firm and true to the vision, as well as her personal integrity.

I also admire how she chose to treat and take care of her family all while building herself as a person and a professional. She remained loyal and consistent to this foundational part of who she is in life.

Our hands write our life story. When you look at your hands, what type of story do they represent?

> When I look at my hands, I see my dad's hands—not feminine hands like most women, but wide and thick, the hands of the son of a working-class farmer. My dad had chores to do every day and night as a kid, and he worked several jobs while playing football and attending college to support a growing family.
>
> I guess the story is that of a strong work ethic, acceptance, gratitude, and thankfulness for what God has given me. *No room for pity or self-loathing.*

At what point in your life did you learn to really know and embrace who you are and choose to live intentionally—in all areas?

> Not until my 40s. I think we are still growing through our early working and child-rearing years and then when you have experiences under your belt and you're trying to raise teenagers, you *really have to be strong in who you are and what you stand for.* That's when kids are needing guidance and strength from their parents, so you have to *be more intentional and consistent in who you are and what you stand for.*
>
> That's true for you both personally and professionally. I think you continue to get more intentional as you age and realize you've got one life to live, and time is running out.

[Continued by . . . Shelly Meighan]

What helped develop your character and your values?

My parents certainly were influential, but in different ways. From my dad, I learned to always give people the benefit of the doubt (you never know their story) and to truly care about seeing others succeed. He did that well as a high school coach.

From my mom, I learned compassion through acts of service. She's always helping someone to this day.

And faith of course. I don't know how you get through life's challenges without having strong faith.

When you look at your life . . .

What has mattered the most? Family, friends, and faith. Your family is unconditional love. Your friends are who keep you strong day to day. *Faith guides you to make the right decisions, even if they aren't the popular ones.*

What has surprised you? How you continue to evolve and gain new and different perspectives as you get older. And that things you might have thought were a big deal when you were younger really aren't *as you see it through the lens of experience and maturity.* How incredibly fast time seems to go as you enter into your last thirty years. This has shocked me and emphasizes the importance of staying healthy.

What would you look at differently? The desire to please others. You realize as you get older that you aren't always doing what's best for someone when all you want is to make them happy. That's as true in the work world as it is for family. And often when you are doing things for others, *you sacrifice something more important like the opportunity to teach. Good leaders learn to let go of things.*

What type of advice would you share with your 30-year-old self?

Speak up more. Don't be afraid to disappoint people. Set goals and revisit them often.

Brilliantly Grounded Wisdom [Prepared by . . . Ursula Pottinga]

Ursula is the co-founder of BEabove Leadership and co-developer of its groundbreaking training program for advanced coaches: Neuroscience, Consciousness, & Transformational Coaching. She is also the CEO of her coaching business, Profound Growth.

While working at the Minneapolis Chamber of Commerce, Ursula ran leadership sessions for our team. I was drawn to her passion and effectiveness to connect with others in such a raw and genuine fashion. She is personally and professionally brilliant.

Our hands write our life story. When you look at your hands, what type of story do they represent?

> My hands are the hands of a potter—they shape the clay (metaphorically speaking, although I'd love to be a potter!), helping me shape each piece of my life and the lives of others, recognizing and accepting that *perfection is in the imperfection.*

> Over the years, I have learned to *get away from the expectation of perfection* by embracing imperfection in myself, and learning to love and embrace the imperfections of others.

> I have learned that I don't have all the answers and when I think I do, life offers me more questions.

At what point in your life did you learn to really know and embrace who you are and choose to live intentionally—in all areas?

> Intentionality is a practice that can be wired into your neural pathways. It strengthens the connection between yourself and what you want. Knowing this, I am a big believer in being intentional.

> Every day, I ask myself . . .

> > *"What do I want to create for this day?"*

> > *"Who do I want to be?"*

> > *"What will be my focus for today?"*

[Continued . . . Ursula Pottinga]

When you set your intentions for the day, your brain, soul, and the universe work together to manifest what you put your attention on.

Intentionality is a tool you need to practice, like every tool available to us. It's not a gimmick!

What helped develop your character and the values you stand for?

All the knocks, bruises, tears, indecisions, disappointments, sleepless nights, fights, failures, challenges, and self-realization brought me to the realization that the bumps and bruises are not ending . . . they are part of life.

Through the hardest parts of life, I learned to reflect, and this reflection helped me to learn and grow.

When you look at your life . . .

What has mattered the most? Love in all forms. Work. Family. Nature. Tennis. Traveling. A glass of wine. The love of God is at my core. Without a spiritual aspect it is impossible to become a fully grounded and joyful person. We must have a belief in something other than ourselves. There must be a bigger purpose.

Each of us was given gifts and blessings not of our own doing, they were *divinely inspired*. Notice what yours are. Live them. *Spend your life and giftedness in areas that are fulfilling and connected to your true calling.*

What has surprised you? I thought I knew what love was, and then I became a grandma. My grandchildren have taught me what unconditional love truly is. My role as a grandparent is not to raise them, provide for them, etc., my only job is to share unconditional love with them. That has changed me. That has filled me. That has brought me to a deeper understanding of what unconditional love is. Now that I know this, I try to bring it to all relationships in life. And the emphasis is in the "trying."

What would you look at differently? I tend to overcommit in the area of work. Because I have always loved every job I have had, this has shown up in every phase of my life.

What I have learned is that I may face the same challenge, yet with each decade my vantage point shifts. I am not looking at it the same way I did in my 30s, 40s, 50s and now late 60s. It's the same problem yet different perspective.

[Continued by . . . Ursula Pottinga]

What type of advice would you share with your 30-year-old self?

Live intentionally. Be present. Right here. Right now. Because you turn around and that year is gone, those ten years are gone. Be present with everything.

Be present as much as you can. There is so much to be gained by being intentional about being present, including *being present when things aren't so great.*

Also, *be aware that your ego wants you to be bigger, better, more of this and that, etc. Be mindful that more is not always better.*

Anything else?

Life is giving you feedback all the time. You do not need a 360-degree assessment to become self-aware. Notice what you bring to environments: Do you create calm or chaos? Do you create harmony or discontent?

Notice. Listen. Observe. *Life is feedback.*

Brilliantly Grounded Wisdom [Prepared by . . . Laurie Stewart]

Laurie is a wife, a dear friend to many, and a professional speaker who travels North America igniting personal growth and leadership in young people.

She is one of the reasons why I do what I do today. Years back, she brought life to an inner curiosity and dream already placed within me. Her passion, charisma, and heart for developing those around her made us naturally connect.

When I launched my business, I sent her a note explaining how she inspired me to do what I do today. And, guess what, thirty years after that spark was formed, she and I often speak and are now entering into a relationship of working in the youth market together. Life aligned our lives again—in a deeply personal and purposeful fashion. It's not by chance!

Our hands write our life story. When you look at your hands, what type of story do they represent?

> Despite trauma, being taught to hide my real self and live out of fear, my hands reach out to people. They represent connection, encouragement, gathering in faith, authenticity, respect, and a commitment to bringing unity.

At what point in your life did you learn to really know and embrace who you are and choose to live intentionally—in all areas?

> When I was 21, I became a Christian. At that time, I knew I was led to be a professional speaker to share my life experiences. Back then, when I chose this path, it was very different. There were very few women speakers, especially at the age of 21. I knew many would advise against this career path—especially at my age—but I still felt compelled to follow my dream.
>
> My journey towards living intentionally really accelerated in the last ten years. In that time, I have truly learned about being intentional, being myself, and being authentic.
>
> My whole life, I have been a very high achiever. I was taught to be perfect and, although I had many accomplishments, I felt insecure. I was believing incorrect things about myself. Intentionally working through past trauma from my childhood, I learned to embrace who I am and who God created me to be.

[Continued by . . . Laurie Stewart]

What helped develop your character and your values?

I was raised with very strong values and in a very authoritarian household. There wasn't much grace, but a lot of authority, which led to my strong self-expectations.

My faith has developed my character, my values system, and enabled me to maintain strong relationships with positive, connected, faithful, and committed people.

When you look at your life . . .

What mattered most? My relationship with my husband, Jeff, others, myself, God, and those I work with. I love using my gifts to serve through the work I have been called to do. At the center of all these relationships is my faith.

Life is all about the right relationships.

What has surprised you? How believing lies about yourself can affect your well-being. You don't need to be perfect, but you need to be excellent in the fashion God created you to be.

What advice would you share with your 30-year-old self?

I would advise myself to always trust God; it's not about pleasing him or others, it's about trust. Trust in him while *moving forward in grace and truth.*

Brilliantly Grounded Wisdom [Prepared by . . . Crystal Knotek]

Crystal is a wife, mother, grandmother, and, professionally, a retired executive with Delta Airlines. She is currently the founder of KLASS cosmetics & skincare and KLASS Act.

My connection with Crystal began while I was consulting with an organization where she served as one of their board members. Crystal is deeply rooted in her core values and oozes a sense of professional savviness and a contagious inner-light and passion.

Our hands write our life story. When you look at your hands, what type of story do they represent?

> I think I continued to grow throughout my life in different areas at different times. However, once I had children, I embraced being a working mom and ensuring they grew up to love Jesus. I wanted to make sure I was being a "corporate missionary."
>
> In other words, holding true to my love and trust in Jesus in all the decisions I made at work. Once I retired, ten years ago, I took a closer look at all areas in my life. I believe I am now focused more than ever on living intentionally—God first, then my husband, family, and serving others.
>
> I do find myself reflecting periodically about my purpose and taking the time to listen to God's guidance: Am I doing what he wants me to be doing?

What helped develop your character and the values you stand for?

> My parents definitely helped me the most. In addition to my husband, more recently my kids are helping me in more ways than I would ever have imagined.
>
> I was also surrounded by amazing co-workers and friends who helped me in many ways professionally and personally.

[Continued by . . . Crystal Knotek]

When you look at your life . . .

What has mattered the most? Faith and family. Currently, building God's businesses with a focus on how we can spread the love of Jesus and help others through our gifts and businesses.

What has surprised you? For many years, I worked for a local airline. The airline merged and, since I didn't want to move my family to Atlanta, my job was eliminated. Throughout the change, I had a co-worker say, "*God's surprises are better than your plans.*" Almost every day I experience how much truth is in that statement and how blessed I am.

What would you look at differently? I would be stronger and bolder in my love for Jesus, both sharing in the workplace and when the kids were younger.

What type of advice would you share with your 30-year-old self?

Love the Lord your God with all your heart, mind, and soul. And hold true to that belief. Take time to read your Bible and do daily devotions. *Listen to what God wants you to do in everything.*

Brilliantly Grounded Wisdom [Prepared by . . . Rod Axtell]

Rod is a husband, father, grandfather, and, professionally, owns a CPA firm.

My involvement with the Minneapolis Chamber of Commerce connected me to Rod. He (along with John) hired me to work for the Chamber. I was fortunate to witness Rod in action as our board chair. I quickly noticed and admired how he handled people and the task(s) at hand.

His influence on my life taught me always to give back to community, to build connections with others by being genuinely interested in them, to listen, to extend grace, to be loyal to family and those who make your life complete and full.

Our hands write our life story. When you look at your hands, what type of story do they represent?

It has been a journey filled with learning, living, and dealing with life's challenges.

As I have matured in age, I have a much better perspective on what is truly important. I still work too many hours and my work-life balance is not aligned the way it should be, but *that is in part who I am*. However, my appreciation for my family and the people that I come in contact with has grown in time, and continues to grow.

At what point in your life did you learn to really know and embrace who you are and choose to live intentionally—in all areas?

At age 50 I walked away from a significant position that was very financially rewarding. However, it did not satisfy my entrepreneurial urge, and I decided to leave the comfort of a career and the ability to coast to retirement.

The journey over the last sixteen-plus years has been personally rewarding, but it could not have been done without the support of my spouse and my daughters.

As I have matured gracefully, the thought of mortality becomes much more real. My legacy is not yet defined, but I know personally the love for my family is most important to me.

[Continued by . . . Rod Axtell]

My faith has gotten stronger, and I've *recognized it's okay not to have all the answers. Prayer is a great way of asking for strength and guidance, and it's a great way to manage stress.*

What helped develop your character and your values?

My parents, siblings, two close uncles, my in-laws, and the small town that I grew up in all shaped me. I started my career knowing the *importance of working hard and being accountable for your decisions.* However, in the end I must give the most recognition to my spouse of forty-six-plus years. Without her support and nurturing, my journey would be one of open space instead of one filled with family and empathy for others.

When you look at your life . . .

What has mattered the most? My family and the people I have been blessed to work with, as well as the clients who have supported me.

What has surprised you? Unintentional leadership skills. It was never my intent (or desire) to be out front, but over time that willingness to volunteer, serve in public office, and *overcome* a stuttering problem has resulted in people looking to me for guidance.

What would you look at differently? In my 30s and 40s I would have spent even more time with my children and my spouse. *I can never get that time back.*

What type of advice would you share with your 30-year-old self?

Be patient and financially conservative without going to an extreme.

Remember what is truly important. It is not your career, the awards or achievements acquired, the amount of money you make, or the size of your home and other tangible stuff. *Success is an individual accomplishment and not measured in dollars and cents.*

[Continued by . . . Rod Axtell]

What is important is your family and friends and how you treat them daily. Success can be measured, in part, by how many people show up at your funeral.

Anything else?

Don't waste your time being angry or second-guessing your decisions that did not work out the way you wanted.

Give people a second chance; *there is "goodness" in everyone.*

Everyone is blessed with special skills. It is up to us to let them know they are appreciated. *You can't say "Thank You" enough if it comes with sincere conviction.*

Brilliantly Grounded Wisdom [Prepared by . . . Michael Varney]

Michael is a father, friend to many, and, professionally, a retired executive in the Chamber of Commerce industry.

I was fortunate to meet Michael when we were on an ACCE (Association of Chamber of Commerce Executives) board together. His experience in the Chamber industry was not the only thing I noticed that made him so memorable. It was the manner in which he interacted with others, as well as how he handled himself. He is a class act leader, respected and liked by all, filled with integrity, always open to lift other leaders within his influence—never feeling threatened or intimidated by anyone, always believing in collaboration and purposeful growth.

Our hands write our life story. When you look at your hands, what type of story do they represent?

> Looking at my hands, I am reminded of the many things they have learned to do over my many years. Early in my school years they learned how to use a keyboard, something my fingers have done millions of times now that I am older. When I was in school, my hands did many things. They drove a school bus for handicapped children. They blistered and were cut and bruised from doing road construction work. They poured drinks as a bartender. I consider my hands to be experienced in many ways, *all of which point to learning and gaining perspective on life.*
>
> As my career took off, I look back on how often *my hands gave younger executives help up the ladder of success.* My hands are most proud of this.

At what point in your life did you learn to really know and embrace who you are and choose to live intentionally—in all areas?

> I think I first learned to chart an intentional path for my life in my late 20s. Mental maturity had finally set in, so I decided to do the things that would make me more valuable to my employer(s), to myself, and to my family. Sadly, it doesn't take much to be better than "average" in most jobs. *No employer seeks "average" talent.* They want first-round draft picks who can really make things happen for them. *I knew I wanted to be something more than average and then invested the time and money,*

[Continued by . . . Michael Varney]

learning how to be better than average. My independent study paid enormous dividends personally and professionally.

What helped develop your character and your values?

Something that is easy for all of us to do is to *take time to actually consider and write down our own core values.* We must *ask ourselves why these values matter* so much and then *commit to living by them.* Companies have their core values. Why not people?

When we are young, we can use our experiences and observations about who we admire and what works in today's workforce to shape our values. *Find the time-tested words from the wisest among us that resonate with who you really want to be.* The *average person will not do this; Winners will.*

When you look at your life . . .

What has mattered the most? I think one of the things that matters most in life is actually the subject of this body of work—*intentionality.* It is my belief that *far too many people drift through life without objectives and a plan to reach them.* The really successful among us *take the time to aspire to greater levels of achievement and then create a plan to make good things happen.*

What has surprised you? Early in my life I was very driven. Setbacks and surprises were interruptions to the journey and somewhat annoying. Over time, I matured and have become aware that *setbacks and surprises are normal parts of the landscape.* They are to be as expected as the occasional red traffic light on the way to the grocery store. The important thing is to stay the course and get to the destination.

What would you look at differently? Youthful energy is great but needs to be handled with care. *Never forget that the people around you really matter.* Family. Friends. Team members at the office. *We are all in this together.* Embracing this notion earlier in life, rather than later, will make the journey both successful and pleasant.

[Continued by . . . Michael Varney]

What type of advice would you share with your 30-year-old self?

I would thank my 30-year-old self for getting its act together and *deciding to be intentional sooner rather than later.* I would also remind my 30-year-old self that life and career are marathons, not sprints. The old cliché about working smarter and not working harder is only partly true. *I think hard work will always be in style. Working hard AND working smart is an unbeatable recipe for success.*

Anything else?

A mentor I had when I was a young executive said something at one of our meetings that really stayed with me. This man was ultra-successful, experienced and respected in his industry, but said something one day that really caught my ear. He said that *everyone has an obligation to earn as much money as possible.* He said that he had actually considered going into a different industry if the compensation warranted doing so.

In an age when earning a lot of money has been vilified and is a subject of derision by the politically correct, this kind of thinking may not seem to be appropriate. But stop and think about it. Most of us work so that the fruits of our labor reward us and our family as well as possible. I've never heard of anyone turning down an increase in compensation from their employer. So, let's get real. *Money does matter, and one of the benefits of being above average at what one does is the compensation that comes with it.*

Brilliantly Grounded Wisdom [Prepared by . . . Jennifer Smith]

Jennifer is a wife, mother, grandmother, and, professionally, the owner of Innovative Office Solutions.

Jennifer has a beautiful personality that instantly pulls you in. Her contagious smile, positive outlook, and heart for others makes you want to be part of her world. When spending time with Jennifer, my experience has been that I always feel bigger after being around her—that's the type of gift she shares with everyone with whom she interacts.

Our hands write our life story. When you look at your hands, what type of story do they represent?

An inspirational adventure filled with adversity and joy.

At what point in your life did you learn to really know and embrace who you are and choose to live intentionally—in all areas?

The biggest turning point in my life was when I was diagnosed with cancer. This was a time of reflection for me and a *chance to live my life more intentionally.*

What helped develop your character and the values you stand for?

My values were set at an early age and were shaped by my parents and my husband. I met my husband in high school, and his values aligned with mine.

When you look at your life . . .

What has mattered the most? My faith, my family, and my work family.

What has surprised you? *My core values have never changed.*

What would you look at differently? Everything that has happened has *helped shaped who I am.*

[Continued . . . Jennifer Smith]

What type of advice would you share with your 30-year-old self?

Be more purposeful!

Brilliantly Grounded Wisdom [Prepared by . . . Randy Kroll]

Randy is a husband, father, grandfather, and, professionally, led a CPA firm for most of his career. After stepping away from that chapter of his life, he became a partner with the Platinum Group.

While working at the Minneapolis Chamber of Commerce, Randy served on our Board of Directors. I have always been impressed with Randy's caring intuition and deep sense for knowing what's right and doing just that. He is a connector of people and passionate about making a difference. He is not only brilliant in business, but with people too.

Our hands write our life story. When you look at your hands, what type of story do they represent?

As I look at my hands, I look at their posture. Are they open? Are they welcoming? Or are they closed or maybe even clenched tightly?

My story reflects my best efforts to *consistently* have opening, welcoming hands—*open to meaningful engagement and dialogue that affirms, encourages, seeks understanding, and learnings that allow others to grow with me with new insights, thoughts, and ideas.* Getting to this place has been a journey—and I confess that I am still on the journey. And that is part of life.

At what point in your life did you learn to really know and embrace who you are and choose to live intentionally—in all areas?

This too has been a journey that has not had an end.

I can identify the beginning of the journey. When I was in my mid-to-late 30s, after reading an impactful book called *Half-Time* by Bob Buford, I recognized that *my heart's desire was to reach a point of significance rather than success.* I had to define that—*what is significant in my life?*

Over time, my contribution to the growth and development of people and organizations became more important in my life than success as measured by position, wealth, or prestige.

[Continued by . . . Randy Kroll]

After reading that book in my mid-to-late 30s, I set a goal to implement a career change when I reached my mid-50s. *This goal inspired me to design* the remaining fifteen years of my original professional life to develop relationships, develop skills, and look forward to something new and good that I was confident was in store for my future.

During this fifteen-year period, *I grew in my intentionality*. And I am still growing in my intentionality—choosing how I want to spend my time serving people and organizations with open, welcoming hands.

What helped develop your character and your values?

My faith has been an integral part of my character development and is the basis for my values as a person and as a professional. How I live out my faith, my character, and my values has been shaped by my interaction with others—the reciprocal nature of relationships. *I have been fortunate to be in relationships with many wise men and women who poured their wisdom into me like a funnel. Listening, exploring, thinking, meditating is all a part of shaping and molding. And with open hands I happily received their wisdom. Now I in turn can generously help others with open hands and shared wisdom.*

When you look at your life . . .

What has mattered the most? Living out my Christian faith in every area of life—family, vocation, relationships—as a friend, counselor, and mentor.

What has surprised you? The *growth I have experienced in periods of significant change and transition when I opened myself up to the new and the unknown,* and how much joy was received in the process.

What would you look at differently? There is always fear of the unknown. I experienced fear as I intentionally lived out a planned transition. The second time was a whole lot less fear-filled. *I would be more confident in who I am, my gifts and abilities, as I face transitions and change.*

[Continued by . . . Randy Kroll]

What type of advice would you share with your 30-year-old self?

Get over yourself as quickly as possible and set your sights on who you want to be, not on what's expected or the desire for more. Then go after it. But *never make life about yourself;* seek the flourishing of others and, in doing so, you will flourish.

Brilliantly Grounded Wisdom [Prepared by . . . Amy Jeatran]

Amy is a wife, mother, and, professionally, a retired business leader

She was introduced to my life during a time when I was heavily involved with Children's Hospitals and Clinics of Minnesota. She and I co-led their largest fundraising gala. It was during that experience that I quickly knew she would become a lifelong friend and mentor.

She and her husband Bill are people that I sincerely admire. Amy has a fashionable style that always makes her look sharp, but what I have grown to adore more than her keen sense for style, in all forms, is her heart. She is professionally savvy yet authentically beautiful—as a person.

At what point in your life did you learn to really know and embrace who you are and choose to live intentionally—in all areas?

There was not "a point" but rather a slow evolution of learning. As I encountered life, family, and career challenges, I quickly learned what I valued most and what was most important in my life. *Once that is defined, living with intention naturally falls into place.* I would add that part of the *evolution of learning is gaining self-awareness, understanding, appreciating your strengths, and acknowledging your weaknesses.* It is with this knowledge that you can make the best choices as you live intentionally.

What helped develop your character and your values?

Many factors have influenced my character and values. Certainly, my parents and extended family were the first and most impactful teachers in my life.

Coming from a family of seven children, we experienced many built-in life lessons: *you are not the center of the universe;* we work as a team and everyone has a job to do; older siblings help the younger ones; hand-me-downs and leftovers fill in the gaps beautifully, etc.

I also grew up in a household (unconventional for that era) where my mom and dad shared the household duties. My dad made dinner, did laundry, put hair in ponytails just as often as my mom. I thought every household was like this. As a result, *I grew up without preconceived roles about who I would become.*

[Continued by . . . Amy Jeatran]

My parents taught us through example to work hard; make sacrifices; an education is essential and can't be taken away; *do your personal best and be kind to others (you do not know their journey)*.

I was blessed to be raised in a home where faith was a part of our everyday life, and I always knew I was loved. I built on this foundation through my life experiences as I married, built a career, balanced children and work, cared for my dad through his illness and death, and experienced the loss of other loved ones.

When you look at your life . . .

What has mattered the most? Relationships, no question! Whether it be relationships with family, friends, co-workers, superiors, or even strangers.

Relationships are at the core of living.

Our interactions with others define our emotions and create our memories. When I look back on life, it is the relationships I share with people that I treasure the most.

What has surprised you? Just how quickly life/time passes.

What type of advice would you share with your 30-year-old self?

- Find a mentor. If I have learned anything, it's that the adage "with age comes wisdom" is so very true! Life experience teaches so much, and those who have walked before you have wisdom to share. So, find a mentor (or two) to provide you guidance in the many facets of life (career, marriage, life balance, personal goals, etc.).
- *Be open-minded and respect differences*! Listen to other's viewpoints, try to see things a different way. You'll be amazed at what you learn and how this will make you so much more "well rounded."
- Take risks. *Step out of your comfort zone.* There truly is no such thing as failure if you learn from the experience and adapt the next time.
- *Carve out time to slow down and be alone.* Your best thinking and healing will come as a result.

[Continued by . . . Amy Jeatran]

- *Treat people with kindness and grace.* In the end, how you treat others is what matters most.
- *Laughter* is amazing therapy. Use it as often as you can. It is the best tool to relieve stress and can cut tension in the worst of circumstances.
- Always know that *you are perfect just as you are.* God made you! You are a unique blend of gifts and skills, challenges and weaknesses. Embrace and love all that you are!

Brilliantly Grounded Wisdom [Prepared by . . . Roger Gjellstad]

Roger is a husband, father, grandfather, and retired owner of Case IH in my hometown of Stanley, North Dakota.

Roger is an active and known leader throughout the community and the state of North Dakota. He has been a friend of my dad's since college and someone I have always admired. He is a solid person who lives his values, professionally and personally—he models leadership in a way that reminds you, "it's always about others."

Our hands write our life story. When you look at your hands, what type of story do they represent?

> When I look at my hands, I think of *hard work*. My father always told us, if you work hard at whatever you do, it will be fine. Hard work results in a job well done, goals accomplished, and satisfaction!

At what point in your life did you learn to really know and embrace who you are and choose to live intentionally—in all areas?

> It was at the age of 25 that I realized I had a hard time working under the supervision of others. I wanted to be my own boss and live a life that I could look back on someday and say "I did it my way." I feel like I accomplished my mission!
>
> I learned that *whatever you do in this life, do it well, and leave it in better condition than when you started.*

What helped develop your character and your values?

> At a younger age, my involvement with sports helped me define my character and accomplish goals early in life. Other school activities and organizations helped me socially—Future Farmers of America being one of them. This club helped me with public speaking, leadership skills, and conducting meetings.
>
> My fraternity in college taught me how to work with people, both professionally and socially. In today's world, most professions involve associating with others.
>
> *The ability to successfully communicate is a tremendous asset.*

[Continued by . . . Roger Gjellstad]

When you look at your life . . .

What has mattered the most? 1) Faith. 2) Family. 3) My job. I was taught this order early on in my career. A man had shared, "To live your life complete, do not ever change that order! If you do, stop and reorganize them back into the original order."

What has surprised you? The biggest surprise is how fast time goes and how fun it can be. *When you surround yourself with others who share the same philosophy as you, it is really fun.*

What would you look at differently? One item that I would have done differently is doing everything myself. *There are others who can help* and probably do it just as well, or even better!

What type of advice would you share with your 30-year-old self?

I would like to be 30 again and take the knowledge I have now and install it back then. I would be more goal-oriented!

If you want it, don't hold back. Plan, forecast, and go for it. *When you accomplish that goal, set another!*

Your capability will surprise you.

Anything else?

When opportunity knocks, answer it! Do not feel that you have to do everything yourself, open up to others.

Do not rely solely on yourself. Have an advisory board, stockholders, or peers to share your ideas. Plus, your banker has to be someone on board with you; always share your ideas with him/her. Hire people who are smarter than you to assist you with your plans. And *most important: Be honest.*

These items will make your life a lot less stressful!

Brilliantly Grounded Wisdom [Prepared by . . . Debb Klingel]

Debb is a widow, mother, grandmother, and, professionally, a retired direct sales executive.

While working at the Minneapolis Chamber of Commerce, I worked for her husband, Todd. Todd has since passed away, yet so much of what he brought to my life remains, including Debb.

The two of them were a remarkable couple. They carried deep belief in themselves which led them to naturally support and encourage each other in a genuine way. They modeled the positive ripple effect that occurs when you are anchored in self-love and belief.

Our hands write our life story. When you look at your hands, what type of story do they represent?

> A story of growth and evolution. I realized early in my career that I got so much joy and satisfaction in helping women find themselves, to see themselves in a positive light, to grow who they are and believe in who they are.

At what point in your life did you learn to really know and embrace who you are and choose to live intentionally—in all areas?

> *I've learned to sit for a minute to see what the reason is for the unexpected shifts or changes in life.*
>
> For example, I was a top direct sales executive for eighteen years with the same company, when I received word they were closing, I moved to another direct sales organization and successfully built that for seven years. When I got the call that they were closing too, I chose to step away and not move into another opportunity.
>
> When I chose to take a step back, my husband Todd was diagnosed with cancer. In front of me was my next job, to take care of Todd, to have my attention, energy, and priorities focused on him.
>
> The door to my business closed because another more important one was opening for which I needed space.

[Continued by . . . Debb Klingel]

Someone learns intentionality if they are fortunate enough *to be around others who are intentional in their thinking and way of living.* Being intentional is a gift that everyone should know.

I would often coach my team, as well as my children, to use certain phrases, to discourage the way of thinking that leaves the door of discouragement open or lack of commitment alive.

"*I intend.*" versus "I want."

"*I will.*" versus "I hope."

"*Do.*" versus "I will try."

When you have an intention, you must have it followed up by a "how" plan. *Your how plan does not have to be complicated, but it should be connected to your why.* Defining your personal mission statement makes you powerful in an intentional fashion.

Be your true self. If you aren't you let other people have the power. If you are not okay on the inside, you are never okay on the outside.

What helped develop your character and your values?

Once you discover what your core values are and what you plan to do with them, you become more aware. Because you are more present in this area, *you work on them all the time without even knowing it.*

When you look at your life. . .

What has mattered the most? I realized early on that *I had the ability to look at every situation and decide how I want to move forward*, regardless of my past or what was modeled to me. In my early 20s I had already started a list of what I wanted my life to be like and already thought about how I wanted it to be shaped.

[Continued by . . . Debb Klingel]

What has surprised you? After losing Todd, people would say, "I bet you never pictured it turning out this way." And "no" I didn't, yet what I have learned is that I can still do this. I have surprised myself with my strength. Just as the saying goes: *You never know how strong you are until being strong is the only choice you have.*

Being strong is a choice. I want to do it for myself, for my kids, and for Todd.

What would you look at differently? I like my life, and the hard times have shaped the good times.

A question Todd often asked is: "*If everyone threw their lives in the middle of the street, whose would you choose?*" If you would not choose your own, why is that? What needs to be changed, shifted, or done differently to make your life the one you would choose?

What type of advice would you share with your 30-year-old self?

Be in the moment.

When we're younger we are distracted all the time—busy getting things done. Don't miss the moments. Show up. Be there!

Anything else?

Learn to communicate honestly and do not be afraid of the answer or response on the other side.

Become aware that there are no accidents in our intelligent universe. Realize that everything that shows up in your life has something to teach you. Appreciate everyone and everything in your life. —Wayne Dyer

Brilliantly Grounded Wisdom [Prepared by . . . Jeri Meola]

Jeri was introduced to my life through my involvement with the National Association of Women Business Owners.

Instantly I was drawn to her genuine smile and compassion for people and life. She is a highly experienced business leader that always is working to help advance what's important to other people. Being around her business savvy and contagious attitude inspires me to lead a life of significance. She models it well!

Our hands write our life story. When you look at your hands, what type of story do they represent?

They represent guidance. They are small hands but have played pivotal stories in my life.

They are the "feelers." My parents would say, "Don't touch; it's hot." I use my hands when I'm speaking to elaborate a point. I use my hands when golfing to help me "feel" the grip and shot.

At what point in your life did you learn to really know and embrace who you are and choose to live intentionally—in all areas?

When my mother told me the one thing you can always be guaranteed in life is "change."

I decided that when I die, I want my gravestone to say "Everyone always wanted to play golf with Jeri." This would fulfill me *living a life with integrity.*

What helped develop your character and your values?

Playing competitive sports. I quickly learned the value of teams and *how to react to stress.*

Being a third-generation women business owner, my grandmother and mother instilled in me many values regarding *how to treat people.* My father always emphasized it's about *"quality, not quantity."* With my older sisters being in the Air Force, *I learned so much about the word "respect" based on their experiences.*

[Continued by . . . Jeri Meola]

When you look at your life . . .

What has mattered the most? Enduring friendships. Having faith. Never doing anything to embarrass my parents. Giving back to the community. Mentoring.

What has surprised you? How cruel of a species we can be.

What would you look at differently? Better understanding of the needs of the next generation. Balance.

What type of advice would you share with your 30-year-old self?

Look at your watch every day and ask yourself, *"Are you spending every minute the way you want?"* Constantly reflect on being the person you want to be.

Every day is a test; it's how *you react* to the test that matters most.

Brilliantly Grounded Wisdom [Prepared by . . . Jane Salmen]

Jane is a wife, mother, and, professionally, the owner/president of Human Capital Partners.

She and I met while I was working for the Minneapolis Chamber of Commerce. Her active role in our organization allowed me to witness her style of leadership and become part of her world.

Her style is always about others. She lives it and surrounds herself with professionals that share the same mindset. What she accomplishes, for herself and others, because of her intentionality in this areas, is pretty rewarding to witness.

Our hands write our life story. When you look at your hands, what type of story do they represent?

> Hard work. Authenticity.

At what point in your life did you learn to really know and embrace who you are and choose to live intentionally—in all areas?

> At the age 37, I had a stroke as a result of a hole in my heart of which I was not aware. I had open-heart surgery to repair the hole.

> My life, goals, aspirations, and dreams changed dramatically. It was a wake-up call for me. *I was given the opportunity to put my priorities in place. Since that time, I live each day intentionally.*

What helped develop your character and your values?

> More than anything, my parents.

> *Strive for goodness, not greatness.* They taught us to *define ourselves by adjectives, not work.* Hard work, compassion, humility, honesty, and kindness were the foundation for their lives.

[Continued by . . . Jane Salmen]

When you look at your life . . .

> **What has mattered most?** Family and friends.
>
> **What has surprised you?** How easily people, myself included, can be sidetracked by those unimportant things in life.
>
> **What would you do differently?** What was important when I was younger is so different than what I value today.

What type of advice would you share with your 30-year-old self?

> Be kind, humble, and generous. *Don't judge others.*

Anything else?

> *Define your own life!*

Brilliantly Grounded Wisdom [Prepared by . . . Dick Bjorklund]

Dick is a husband, father, grandfather, and, professionally, he runs a thriving financial services practice at Principal Financial Group.

While working for Principal, I met Dick and was drawn to his style of expansion. His outlook on growth is always about serving others. This genuine attitude has made him wildly successful, and it also has lifted the people around him to higher levels of effectiveness, productivity, and self-worth. He champions growth in a transformational fashion.

Our hands write our life story. When you look at your hands, what type of story do they represent?

> The story is one of *genuinely embracing my passion of helping people.* Being part of the financial services business has allowed me to do that daily. That passion extends beyond business as my wife, Kris, and I are also involved in many charitable causes.

> Early in my career I was helped by so many other advisors who shared their passions and experience freely, forming an attitude that we are a team, not in competition with each other.

> *I adopted the give back mantra very early because of this spirit.*

> My father led the Minnesota Business Center years back and, with the help of many, built an amazing culture. He was an unbelievable role model to have.

When you look at your life, what has mattered most?

> Family and friends are the most important aspect of life and always come first. I feel honored to be in a business that allows me to make that happen every day.

> As I look back, I can say that I have no regrets or changes to make. I have been the recipient of great help and advice from so many amazing people. A special acknowledgment goes to my partner on this journey, Kris Bjorklund. Without her it would not have happened. She is amazing.

Brilliantly Grounded Wisdom [Prepared by . . . Kim Plahn]

Kim is a wife, mother, and, professionally, the president of Dunn Brothers Coffee.

When Kim and I met a handful of years ago through Women Presidents' Organization, I gravitated to her witty style in business, as well as her kind and helpful heart. She has a strong sense of discernment for right from wrong and great courage to use her internal anchors to guide her. I absolutely admire that in her, as well as how she handles the people side of life and business.

Our hands write our life story. When you look at your hands, what type of story do they represent?

> When I look at my hands, they represent a life that has been lived fully—a life that has purpose, love, family, friendships, and hardships. Hands that listen, learn, provide guidance, care, and love.
>
> *Those hands may look polished and cared for from afar, but as you look closely they are calloused and weathered from hard work and perseverance.*

At what point in your life did you learn to really know and embrace who you are and choose to live intentionally—in all areas?

> I was in my late 20s to early 30s, I was married and having children, and a vice president of a public company. Life was filled with many incredible people, yet it was so busy and demanding.
>
> It was at this point that I really *had to decide to be content with the choices I made.*
>
> There were times in my work life that others would try to push me beyond my ethical boundaries. I knew every morning I needed to get up and look in the mirror and be accountable to myself and my family, and be proud of those choices. *That was the point in my life that I became okay with myself and knew that the decisions were mine to be made.*

What helped develop your character and your values?

Growing up, my family supported who I am today. I was also told that there were no limits to who I could be or what I could do, and *I believed that*. I grew up confident, curious, competitive, caring, and loving life.

When you look at your life . . .

What has mattered the most? My family.

What has surprised you? How fast time has gone. I realize now as I am nearing 60 that life will be changing. I will need to *surround myself with those things that fill my soul* for the next twenty to thirty years.

What would you look at differently? Make sure to take time to *slow down enough to enjoy yourself and those around you today*. You do not always know what tomorrow will bring.

What type of advice would you share with your 30-year-old self?

Remain curious, give to others, *find those things that bring you joy, and live your life proud*. You will be pushed beyond your limits, but *do not be afraid to take some risks and be uncomfortable*. That is how we all grow.

Anything else?

It is a wonderful world, yet *we can all make it better!*

Brilliantly Grounded Wisdom [Prepared by . . . Carey Lindeman]

Carey is another special friend I met through my time at Women Presidents' Organization. She is a mother, and, professionally, the founder and president of Promise Care, Inc.

In my time with her I have always admired her deep desire to be true to who she is, as well to those she embraces through her work. She is caring, compassionate, and filled with a wealth of knowledge and life experiences.

Our hands write our life story. When you look at your hands, what type of story do they represent?

> My hands represent years of caring for others, using touch to comfort, console, and ease the pain of sickness, aging, and going through the dying process.

At what point in your life did you learn to really know and embrace who you are and choose to live intentionally—in all areas?

> When my children were grown to a point where they possessed *habits and values that were going to serve them well in life.* At that time I discovered, through a ministry at church, a new direction—to pursue a career in caring for others and developing a unique business around it.

What helped develop your character and your values?

> I had a good upbringing that taught me the values I stand for today. At the age of 35, I became deeply involved with Bible study and from that point I *have used the Bible as my guide for life.* This has helped me deepen my values, which helped me create a mission for my business, family, and relationships.

When you look at your life . . .

> **What has mattered the most?** People. *Learning to accept them where and as they are,* whether it's children, clients, friends, or people I meet for the first time.

> **What has surprised you?** *Everyone has a very unique story.*

[Continued by . . . Carey Lindeman]

What would you look at differently? My finances. I wish I had been more intentional about my finances through my life and used the wonderful resources that are available so I could make even more of a difference today.

What type of advice would you share with your 30-year-old self?

Don't think you know it all. *Always be open to help from others.*

Anything else? *Spend less. Give more.*

Brilliantly Grounded Wisdom [Prepared by . . . Michael Geis]

Michael is a husband, father, grandfather, and, professionally, the founder and president of The Geis Group.

Michael and I met while I was serving on various committees at Children's Hospitals and Clinics of Minnesota,. He was a legacy planning consultant for the foundation team. We instantly connected as people, and I have grown to truly admire his style, experience, and the way in which he guides people through personal planning chapters in their lives. He is a mentor and friend.

When you look at your hands, what type of story do they represent?

My hands are indicative of my life's journey. Most noticeable are the visible scars from numerous scrapes and scuffs associated with farm life and lifelong use of tools. Evident are signs of skin damage due to sun exposure. Protruding and obvious veins are symbolic of my active pursuits professionally and personally. Bent fingers and enlarged knuckles reveal arthritis, although my hands continue to work in fine precision.

My hands have been the entry point for countless relationships that resulted from a first-hand shake. My life has been a people business offset with a passion for restoring old, broken, or damaged items. People tell me my hands resemble those of someone laboring outdoors and not what they presume befitting of someone in professional services.

My hands have enabled me to enjoy an equal balance in right/left brain tasks.

At what point did you learn to really know and embrace who you are and choose to live intentionally—in all areas?

At 55 years of age, I started The Geis Group. Being my own boss was always in my thoughts, but it wasn't until I amassed enough experience that radiated competence and proficiency to instill confidence in prospects that I made the leap. *Failure was never a consideration,* which perhaps explains why I was not deterred from launching in less than positive economic times.

[Continued by . . . Michael Geis]

My goal was to *differentiate myself* from all other fundraising consultants, to meet clients where they were instead of forcing one model fits all. I committed to the philosophy of under-promising and over-delivering. Other than an expensive ad I placed in a trade journal my first year, I have never advertised, and we exist today extensively through referrals and renewals.

What helped you develop your character and your values?

Growing up on a farm with seven siblings had everything to do with whom I've become.

Performing daily chores and shouldering responsibilities for operating complex machinery, when your feet barely reach the clutch, accelerates maturity like forcing diesel fuel into a turbocharged engine.

Spending summers on my uncle's dairy farm during my formative years instilled a strong work ethic. *I always believed I could outwork anyone else.* When town kids helped with bailing hay, I made them earn the extra $.25 per hour my uncle offered. When I asked my mother, "Who was the smartest of her eight children," her response was, "I don't know, but *you might be the most tenacious.*"

Sports were also instrumental in formulating my character. My achievements were not attributable to exceptional athletic ability but instead an insatiable desire to outperform my competition. Sports instilled the *value of leadership and teamwork.*

When you look at your life . . .

What has mattered the most? Nothing gives me greater pride than my family. *They deliver daily doses of happiness.* I delight in their achievements and cheer for them as a parent.

It was my wife who started praying early in our marriage for two outcomes with our children—that they would find wonderful lifelong mates and that they would enjoy each other's company throughout their adult lives. So far so good!

[Continued by . . . Michael Geis]

What has surprised you? The pace of time accelerates as we age. The older I get, the faster time spins. Days seem like minutes and months like hours. I've also learned from assisting literally thousands with their estate plans that *people are people regardless of where they live.* At the center of most people's lives are their families. *Everyone I've worked with wants what's best for their family and endeavors to provide for them in the most optimal manner.*

What would you look at differently? I would have pursued business or entrepreneurial ventures to a greater extent. I learned later in life that I have a passion for starting businesses and enjoy daily the benefits and challenges of seeing The Geis Group, Assay, and Geis Properties evolve.

What advice would you share with your 30-year-old self?

- Surround yourself with friends and acquaintances that infuse positivity into your life and actively seek time with them.
- Recruit a board of directors that can nurture, mentor, affirm, and challenge you to achieve your optimal self personally and professionally.
- Develop a prayer life that's in balance with other life priorities.
- Exercise regularly and eat right.
- Love your family every minute, and never leave them wondering what you think of them.
- Write more letters and notes to those who matter to you.
- Read and pursue interests outside of your work focus.
- Be more collaborative and foster individual ownership and authorship as it relates to problem-solving at work and at home.
- Exercise random kindness daily.
- Nurture a talent and interest that would surprise most people.
- Laugh more often.

Brilliantly Grounded Wisdom [Prepared by . . . Maureen Bausch]

Maureen is a wife, mother, and, professionally, a founding partner of Bold North Associates. She was an executive at the Mall of America for most of her career before taking on the responsibility of CEO for the LII Super Bowl Host Committee.

Maureen is one of the most gracious, humble, and brilliant leaders with whom I have spent time. She absolutely knows who she is from her inner core, and when you spend time with her you feel it. She is a leader who holds firm and brings people to higher levels with her.

Our hands write our life story. When you look at your hands, what type of story do they represent?

> Hard work—very hard work. They resemble both of my grandmothers' hands. I hope I have even half their wisdom.

At what point in your life did you learn to really know and embrace who you are and choose to live intentionally—in all areas?

> In 1990 when I moved from Cub Foods to the Mall of America. At Cub I fell into the work and learned that I loved it.
>
> When I got the job at the Mall of America, I was able to take everything I learned and could start fresh with it. I had very good role models who I wanted to emulate. I was very intentional and knew how I wanted to operate as a professional—it was my choice to decide how I wanted to conduct myself. My role models helped form that image.
>
> The most important part about business and life are the relationships. People stay with you when they know you are real and care. Your relationships last a lifetime. It's important to understand the value of your friendships and business relationships.
>
> I was at the Mall of America from the beginning. Most people at that time did not believe the mall would succeed. They did not understand the concept of entertainment and shopping under one roof, and thought of us as outsiders building something unnecessary. Through intentional relationship building, education, and understanding, we convinced people to visit. We knew that if we could entertain them at least once, they would enjoy themselves and come back. In all relationship building there needs to be trust. Even if you want people to visit, they need to trust that it will be a good experience.

[Continued by . . . Maureen Bausch]

What helped develop your character and your values?

I was lucky. My parents, grandparents, and extended family were extremely good role models. They had very high ethical and moral values. They provided *strong roots yet the wings to fly.* (I'm not sure who wrote that, but I carried it with me for years when raising my own children because it best described how I was raised.)

When you look at your life . . .

What has mattered the most? Family and friends, by far.

What has surprised you? Every once in a while—even after all these years—I meet a dishonest person or mean person. It still shocks me. I have seen these behaviors destroy a great corporate culture and ruin a business.

I have avoided these people sometimes by directly challenging them and always by "giving off a vibe" that I do not agree with their strategy. Speaking up is not the most popular tactic, however it is sometimes necessary for the greater good. Each situation is different.

What would you look at differently? To have had my children earlier in life because I want to see and spend time with my grandchildren. I also potentially would have switched jobs more frequently because in doing so, you're able to work with a variety of industries. That said, at the Mall of America I was able to work with hundreds of retail, restaurant, service, and entertainment brands.

What type of advice would you share with your 30-year-old self?

Be true to yourself. You know what kind of person you want to be—go be it.

Don't do things that make you feel bad.

Fail fast. *No one gets through life without mistakes.* It is how you recover/makeup from those mistakes that matters.

Anything else?

Everything is a moment in time.

Brilliantly Grounded Wisdom [Prepared by . . . Jennifer Sayre]

Jennifer is a wife, mother, grandmother, and, professionally, a key executive with Delta Airlines.

Jennifer and I met while she was serving on the Board of Directors at the Minneapolis Regional Chamber of Commerce. She quickly became a leader that I found myself gravitating toward. I naturally connected with her positive and kind spirit. Throughout the years, she has become a dear friend and mentor—teaching me lasting lessons about the art of blending my professional life with my role as a wife and mother, and to never chase after success at the expense of those who need us the most.

Our hands write our life story. When you look at your hands, what type of story do they represent?

> To be honest, this first question scared me a bit. I don't know that I'm that reflective to stare at my hands and see anything but just hands . . . and old hands now! However, when I do try and reflect on my hands writing my life story, I get emotional.
>
> I think of holding my mom's and dad's hands as a little girl, trusting wherever they would take me. I think of the first time holding the hand of my husband (at age 16), and again trusting this was the right person for me. I think of holding both of my kids in my hands for the first time and trusting God is with me and will help me to raise them. Finally, I think of holding my granddaughter and being overwhelmed with gratitude for the blessings God has given my family.
>
> My hands represent my life as a daughter, wife, mother, and grandmother who is grateful for God and my faith and my family.

At what point in your life did you learn to really know and embrace who you are and choose to live intentional—in all areas?

> This is a work in progress. I feel that in *each stage of life you learn more about yourself and embrace each new development.*
>
> From a young age, I *intentionally strived to have a positive outlook on life every day.* I have a saying on my desk: *When you get up in the morning, you have two choices— either to be happy or to be unhappy. Just choose to be happy.*

[Continued by . . . Jennifer Sayre]

I also intentionally take *time to unwind and recharge. There's more to life than just work.* We must make it a point to enjoy our lives every day doing something we love. Spending time with family, exercising, and restoring myself spiritually is what I enjoy. This helps to make me well-rounded and to be a better employee, wife, mother, and grandmother.

What helped develop your character and the values you stand for?

My parents helped develop my character and the values that I stand for. I often say, they are my number one fans!

My dad has been my business mentor throughout my forty-year career. He always instilled enthusiasm and the importance of giving 110 percent to everything you do. He was a long-time executive for Dayton's, and early in his career a colleague shared a saying that he framed and had in his office all his career and passed it on to his children and grandchildren. This saying has been in my office all my career as well.

ENTHUSIASM!

ENTHUSIASM – the maker of friends, the maker of smiles, the producer of confidence. It cries to the world, "I've got what it takes."

ENTHUSIASM – the inspiration that makes you "wake up and live." It puts spring in your step, spring in your heart, a twinkle in your eye, and confidence in yourself and your fellow men.

ENTHUSIASM – it changes a dead-pan salesman to a producer, a pessimist to an optimist, a loafer to a go-getter.

ENTHUSIASM – if you have it, show it! Your prospect gets it. Your company loves it and you cash in on it.

ENTHUSIASM – do you have it? Then thank God for it. If you haven't got it, then get down on your knees and pray for it.

Upon the plains of hesitation, bleached the bones of countless millions who, on the threshold of victory, sat down to wait, and waiting, they died.

My dad, who is 90 this year, still has this saying on the wall and mentions it often to his grandchildren as they are rising in their careers. His other motto, which has served us well is: *"Do something new that no one else has ever done at your job."* I consider this to include—*continue to learn new things and stay curious!*

My mom, who is 87 this year, has been my spiritual mentor throughout my life. She has implanted the importance of God and faith in my life, which has always been with me throughout my life both in business and raising a family. One of her favorite Bible verses has become mine, too, and has been taped on my computer or laptop to keep me grounded:

> *Do not be anxious about anything, but in every situation, by prayer and petition, with thanksgiving, present your requests to God. And the peace of God, which transcends all understanding, will guard your hearts and your minds in Christ Jesus.* –Philippians 4:6-7

My parents encouraged me throughout my life, supporting me when I needed reassurance that I could handle being a good wife and mother while balancing the demands of a challenging career. This everlasting support has developed core values in me such as trust, honesty, and commitment, which I apply to all areas of my life, at work and at home.

When you look at your life . . .

What has mattered the most? My family has mattered most. I am blessed in so many ways when it comes to family. I married my high-school sweetheart. His encouragement and support of my goals throughout our lives has been a game-changer. My success in business has been a joint accomplishment. It's important to support each other. We have two wonderful children close by, and a precious granddaughter and grandson on the way. *I've had many successes in my life, but none compare to the joy my family brings me.*

Now that I near retirement, many ask, "Where are you going to live, or what are you going to do?" Again, that's an easy answer: "I'm going to live by my children and grandchildren, and I'm going to do things to support and encourage them!"

[Continued by . . . Jennifer Sayre]

What has surprised you?

I am surprised at what you can do when you get out of your comfort zone! I remember being asked to represent my company on Chamber of Commerce Boards which was totally outside my area of expertise. However, I welcomed the opportunity as a new challenge and chance to expand my responsibilities. I was very nervous and initially felt very inferior to my prominent fellow board members. I spent many years on these Boards and ended up chairing the Foundation Board and several committees. These appointments required frequent speaking engagements in front of both small and large meetings. I was petrified in the beginning but worked my way up to being only partially petrified in the end . . . it became more exciting than intimidating. *I never thought that I would be able to do this, but if you believe in yourself, you can do anything!*

What would you look at differently?

I would have tried earlier not to worry about things you cannot control. Also, not to worry about what I thought others were thinking. Both practices are unhealthy and create negativity. I'd be less guilty about not having enough time to do everything. In the end when I look back at my life so far, I achieved a work and life balance which is so important.

I would also take time to keep or rekindle old relationships that have been lost. *We get so busy doing life that some treasured relationships fall by the wayside.* I have recently renewed a few old college relationships and am thrilled to have these friends in my life again.

What type of advice would you share with your 30-year-old self?

I would tell my 30-year-old self to *be more present and enjoy the journey.* Not that I did not enjoy the journey, because I have; however, I do believe I rushed through my 30s and 40s with the stress of young children and the demands of corporate life. I can remember the stress of rushing from work to kid's functions and feeling that I couldn't wait for these obligations to be over. Now, I think back on these and miss them. *Don't rush to check the event off the "to-do" list, go there and enjoy it and savor the*

[Continued by . . . Jennifer Sayre]

moment.

On the positive side, I did enjoy the journey, breaking norms by bringing my young children to business meetings around the world. I was initially worried about them missing school, but the benefits of these trips together and the educational opportunities were priceless.

Moral of the story: *Do what feels right and you won't regret it!*

The image on the back cover is one of a *Mandala*.

A mandala represents wholeness and symbolizes an individual's journey and path in life.

It's primarily used to help people journey inward to gain wisdom and explore their thoughts from within—perfect for the work of this guide.

It is our sincere hope that this interactive book sparked an inside out connection for you, in a fashion that's *original* and *authentic* to who you are—inspiring you to **own** *your true brand of brilliance!*

You know how every once-in-a-while you do something and the little voice inside says, "There. That's it. That's why you're here." . . . and you get a warm glow in your heart because you know it's true? Do more of that. —Joseph Nodby

You. *Defined!*
Dare to go within . . . to *Define* what you want . . . to show up as *YOU!*
www.bar33leadership.com